Reviewer Information

WINNING BY TELEPHONE: Telephone Effectiveness for Business Professionals and Consumers

by Gary S. Goodman

144 pages $7.95

Please forward two copies of all reviews.

PRENTICE-HALL, INC., Englewood Cliffs, N.J. 07632

Winning by Telephone: Telephone Effectiveness for Business Professionals and Consumers by Gary S. Goodman

Address inquiries to Prentice-Hall, Inc.,
Englewood Cliffs, N.J. 07632
Printed in the United States of America
Prentice-Hall International, Inc., London
Prentice-Hall of Australia, Pty. Ltd., Sydney
Prentice-Hall of Canada, Ltd., Toronto
Prentice-Hall of India Private Ltd., New Delhi
Prentice-Hall of Japan, Inc., Tokyo
Prentice-Hall of Southeast Asia Pte. Ltd., Singapore
Whitehall Books Limited, Wellington, New Zealand

10 9 8 7 6 5 4 3 2 1

ISBN 0-13-960971-7

ISBN 0-13-960963-6 {PBK.}

Library of Congress Cataloging in Publication Data

Goodman, Gary S.
Winning by telephone.
Includes index.
1. Telephone in business. 2. Telephone etiquette.
I. Title.
HE8735.G66 658.4'52 81-23556
ISBN 0-13-960971-7 AACR2
ISBN 0-13-960963-6 (pbk.)

This book is dedicated to my wife, Deanne; to the memory of my father, Bernard Goodman; and to the memory of Roy Honeyman.

Acknowledgments

A number of people have been influential in my experience in the field of telephone effectiveness. To an early booster and inspirational boss, Larry Kramer, of Westlake Village, California, and formerly of Time/Life Books, Inc., I owe a special word of thanks. He believed in my abilities and gave me a rare opportunity to test them at an early stage in my professional development.

I would also like to thank the educators who have helped me to appreciate human communication from theoretical perspectives. My thanks go to Dr. Fred McMahon, of California State University, Northridge; Dr. James McBath, Dr. Kenneth K. Sereno, Dr. Walter Fisher, and Dr. Janet Bolton, of the University of Southern California.

Acknowledgments should be made to the scores of universities and organizations that have sponsored my Telephone Effectiveness, Telephone Marketing, and Customer Relations seminars throughout the nation. At the top of the list is Indiana State University and its great staff in Conferences, Non-Credit Programs, and Continuing Education.

The inspiration and assistance of my wife and partner, Professor Deanne Honeyman-Goodman, of California State University, Los Angeles, has been enormous. It is to her that I offer the most special appreciation.

Introduction

According to San Francisco Bell Telephone statisticians in "Openline," the average American spends a total of 8,760 hours on the phone in an average life-span of seventy years. This amounts to an entire year of our lives!

Is that year well spent for most of us? How many people can truly say that they get the most out of every telephone call they make or take? Judging from the testimony of thousands of folks who have attended my Telephone Effectiveness and Customer Relations seminars across the country, the answer is very few, indeed. In fact, according to researchers, most people have an ambivalent, if not negative, attitude toward using the phone.

This book combines twelve years of experience in telephone communication management, training, and consultation with insights derived from behavioral research to give the reader practical tips for developing telephone effectiveness. Business communications are emphasized in a number of chapters, and a special section (Chapter 6) is devoted to helping consumers "fight back by telephone."

It is my hope that this book will be a guide for becoming more productive with a medium that *Dun & Bradstreet Reports* calls the "hottest communications tool around."

As you leaf through these pages, you will be listening not only to the voice of the author but to the distilled wisdom and insights of thousands of folks around the country who use the telephone as their number-one professional tool. It is to their ingenuity and helpfulness that I owe a special word of thanks.

Gary S. Goodman, Ph.D.
Glendale, California

Contents

WINNING
BY
TELEPHONE

1

Tele-Time Management

A journalist once asked me during an interview why I find the telephone such an exciting tool when most folks regard it as just another piece of furniture. I immediately said that I would never have been able to accomplish what I had in terms of starting a business and developing markets throughout the country if the telephone had been unavailable to me. If I had relied upon more traditional means of starting a consulting business, I would have invested (and probably lost) thousands of dollars on mailers and display advertisements and creating local "goodwill" through the employment of expensive publicists. The telephone was clearly the best, the least expensive, and the most timely means of influencing decision makers. Not everyone, however, shares my enthusiasm for the phone as a time-management device.

Time-Maker or Time-Waster?

If we ask people to name an activity that wastes more of their time on the job than other activities, frequently we will hear the reply, "Talking on the phone." Many folks regard the telephone as their worst "interruption," especially when they are trying to accomplish something "important." Feelings about using the phone can be extremely negative, as some studies have shown.

According to one study, over 15 percent of the respondents to a questionnaire said they "avoid using the telephone as much as possible" or indicated that they "dislike using the phone but use it when necessary." A hefty number of people indicated that they "use the telephone whenever they have to," but this contingent of 51 percent expressed no positive attitudes about using this business tool. Only a third said they "enjoy using the telephone and use it at every opportunity."[1]

This study is significant because it tells us that the telephone is not the first choice of communication channels for a large number of users. Nevertheless, we are all going to be using the telephone more to save time, energy, and fuel, as these precious resources dwindle. A glimpse into the future tells us that the phone will become our indispensable link to the world of information and the world of work.

Toward Telecommunity: Dialing to Work

Alvin Toffler, the noted author and futurist, points out that many of us are already "telecommuting" to work, rather than wasting time and other resources by driving through clogged arteries to our places of employment. He predicts that more and more of us will use the telephone and telephone lines via computer to link ourselves with our clients and business associates.[2]

As our society completes its historic transformation from an agricultural and industrial orientation to an "information" orientation, many will think of work as a matter of receiving, shaping, and transmitting information, rather than as a place we go to in the morning.

Becoming Tele-Time Managers

Given the increasing importance of the telephone, how may we best manage our time through its use? How may we inconspicuously control our conversations so we are not victimized by the "blabbers" and "ramblers" who will not gracefully bring conversations to their conclusions? How may we best gather information without being put on hold, and how may we overcome the habit of having to make call-backs because we "forgot just one little thing" during the last call? What are some of the subtle tips we can use to make our voices more effective in stating our business in a succinct, yet friendly way? What methods may be used to plan our conversations and make easily understood and easily retrieved records for later review and reference?

Planning

I suspect much of the dissatisfaction expressed by telephone users results from the fact that phone conversations are usually unplanned, wandering affairs. It is not surprising that we fail as often as we do in achieving our telephonic objectives for the simple reason that we do not clearly state our objectives to ourselves before dialing, and we do not refer to these goals after the conversation has begun. It's easy to get lost when we don't know where we are headed.

We also tend to be disappointed with the way our phone calls proceed because we somehow feel as though we have "lost control" of the subject matter, the attention of the listener, or the other party's delivery or conversational style.

These problems are remedied through the use of vocal nuances and call planning.

Rule 1: Control the Conversation with Your Voice and Delivery

Many of us subscribe to the popular ethic that telephone conversations, like face-to-face exchanges, should be rather democratically conducted in a give-and-take fashion. Although this is a "nice" goal or ideal for which to strive, it is not a prerequisite for having a successful conversation. In some cases, in fact, it can get in the way. Success may require we "tell it like it is," in a crisp, controlled fashion. To do so, we must be prepared to orchestrate our delivery as well as that of our counterpart on the other end of the line.

"Just When You Thought It Was Safe to Talk on the Phone . . ."

Some folks seem to use every opportunity to waste our time on the phone. One culprit is known as "Jaws."

Jaws is the person who simply cannot wait until we are finished speaking to introduce his ideas into the call. We can hear him rushing toward us as he tries to speed us up with a flurry of "I knows" and "uh-huhs," while hoping that this artificial feedback will give him the right to speak again. What do we do when we sense that Jaws is after us? We do ourselves in by speeding up, by doing what this fellow wants.

This is the way it works on the phone. We fear that we are going to be interrupted by an impatient or otherwise aggressive person. To avoid this, we speed up and try to compress our ideas into a thimble. When Jaws senses our alarm, he comes in for the kill.

Speakers interrupt us when they think we have come to the end of a thought. This usually occurs when we arrive at the end of a sentence because we normally pause for air at that time before proceeding with our next sentence or idea. We have to breathe, don't we?

Take a Tip from . . . Uh . . . John Wayne . . . Pilgrim!

Several years ago, John Wayne mentioned that he used only one acting technique consciously. He developed the habit of *pausing in a strategic way after certain words in order to make what he was saying sound more interesting to the audience.* This technique was the most distinctive quality of the Duke's delivery—the one nuance that impressionists seize to create their imitations. By pausing as he did, John Wayne riveted generations of moviegoers to their seats.

For our purpose, what the Duke was doing was *pausing for air in the middle of a sentence, rather than at the end of the sentence.* This helped him to control the interest of the audience, and it works on the telephone to help us control the conversation. When we pause in this fashion, we are able to accomplish many things at one time. First, we can luxuriate in a longer pause than otherwise because we have the attention of the listener who wants to hear us complete our thought. Second, we will be developing momentum as we move from phrase to phrase, not "stopping" for the punctuation. One idea will feel as if it is blending with the next in a smooth fashion. With this kind of "steam" built up, it becomes increasingly difficult for anyone to interrupt us unless we wish to relinquish control of the communication channel. We will be covering more information than we would otherwise within the time available. If done correctly, we *will not appear to be rushing, but on the contrary, will sound composed and more assured.*

As with any new communication technique, this sort of procedure takes time and practice in order to produce proficiency. I suggest you first work with a tape recorder and any book. Turn on the tape and read one paragraph from the book as you normally would, pausing at the ends of sentences before moving on to the next. Without turning off the recorder, read the same paragraph, this time pausing *in the middle of each sentence and not stopping at the punctuation marks.* Repeat this procedure with several pages of the book.

You will probably find that this technique feels "weird" or a little strange at first. This is to be expected. After a while, you will no doubt notice that you are able to do this with greater and greater ease, *without altering the meanings you hope to arouse through the sentences.*

Regaining Control When You've Lost It

Sometimes our best-planned telephone calls will get sidetracked. The other person, for one reason or other, will get off the subject or speak at excessive length about a given matter. How can we regain control of the conversation in order to say a few important words ourselves?

If we simply try to commandeer the call by talking above the other person's speech, we will make the person angry, and rightly so, because this behavior is rude. To avoid making the other person uncomfortable, we need to bridge from his or her tangent to what we wish to say. Our bridge, or *transition phrase,* should show we are interested in what the other person has been saying, at the same time indicating there has been a shift in the flow of the call.

Several transition phrases work well in helping us assert control over the call in a friendly way. They are:

1. *WELL, I UNDERSTAND THAT, BUT . . .*
2. *WELL, I APPRECIATE THAT, THOUGH . . .*
3. *WELL, I RESPECT THAT, HOWEVER . . .*
4. *WELL, I KNOW WHAT YOU MEAN, BUT . . .*
5. *WELL, I'D BE SURPRISED IF YOU WERE AT THIS POINT, BUT . . .*

Transition phrases are easy to insert into a conversation. They are used precisely at the end of a phrase, thought, or sentence uttered by the other party. We say the line and then bridge back to the matter at hand or to our preferred subject. Here is an example of a transition phrase in action:

> Caller: *I thought that was probably the worst thing they could have done at that point. Right away, I said to myself that I wasn't going to give them any more of my business!*
>
> Gary: *WELL, I'D BE SURPRISED IF YOU WERE AT THAT POINT, BUT there were a few things I hoped to cover with you about the Frisbee account. First . . .*

In this example any of the transition phrases above would have worked to bridge from the other person's monologue to our talk. We could have easily substituted in this fashion:

> Gary: *WELL, I RESPECT THAT. HOWEVER, there were a few things I hoped to cover with you about the Frisbee account. First . . .*

Why are transition phrases so effective in returning control of conversations to us? They work in a few ways. We begin to interrupt the other person by *first agreeing with him or her.* This is crucial because we are being diplomatic as we divert the flow of the call. We also use *ego-pleasing language* by telling the other party that we are *understanding, appreciating, respecting, knowing, and identifying with THEM.* After having "paid our dues" in these ways, we have "earned the right" to say what is on our minds.

As long as the basic pattern of the transition phrase is used, you are free to invent your own variants of these lines. For instance, some folks like these related phrases:

> *WELL, I AGREE WITH YOU, THOUGH . . .*
> *WELL, THAT'S HAPPENED TO ME TOO, YET . . .*
> *WELL, THERE'S A LOT OF TRUTH IN THAT, AND . . .*
> *WELL, THAT'S INTERESTING, BUT . . .*
> *WELL, WHAT DO YOU KNOW . . .*

Using Various Excuses: "Gotta Run!"

Many of us are victimized by our own good manners and civility. We will find ourselves hopelessly locked into a conversation with a long-winded bore and yet feel bound to continue the call for fear that cutting it short may appear rude to the other person. Out of frustration and necessity, we often fabricate excuses to end the calls in a swift fashion.

To say, "I'm sorry, I have another line ringing," or, "I have a two o'clock appointment waiting for me," or "I have a long-distance call holding for me," is perfectly acceptable in order to manage your time.

Some excuses are better than others. The time-worn lines that many of us use at home are transparent to the other party and should be avoided. They are: "I think there is somebody at the door," and "I think something is burning in the oven!" Rather than giving us control of the call in an inconspicuous fashion, they signal the other party that we have lost control and are clumsily searching for any excuse to terminate the call.

Managing Outward: Drawing Out Their Conclusion

There is a concept in business management theory known as "managing upward." It suggests that we often find ourselves in organizations in the position of having to manage our supervisors and superiors in order to accomplish our objectives. We normally think about the influence process as working in the other direction, from superior to subordinate.

Similarly, on telephone calls, we occasionally find ourselves in the position of having to *manage outward* by influencing the way the other party is expressing a point. In other words, we sometimes have to *help the other party to express his or her ideas in a more organized, concise fashion, without bringing attention to what we are doing.* One of the best ways to accomplish this is to draw a conclusion for the other party before he or she gets around to doing so.

Gary: *It sounds to me like it was rough going for a while.*

Caller: *Yes, it was, in fact. . . .*

Gary: *Well, let's see what the next step is in getting our project off the ground. I was . . .*

Another approach to summarizing the call and inducing the other party to be succinct is to *get clarity on what you have covered or agreed to so far.* A few phrases are helpful here:

Gary: *Well, let's see where we have come so far. . .*

or

Fine, now just so we're clear, we've decided to . . .

These phrases alert the other person that the call is concluding and at the same time gives us an opportunity to verify the substance of understandings that have been created during the call.

Rule 2: Manage Your Time by Outlining Your Calls

Call planning is essential to effective time management by telephone. Unfortunately, most business people with whom I have interacted through seminars and consulting admit that they use no formal system for outlining the subject areas they wish to cover during conversations. This leaves them in the position of having to extemporize what they are saying, which leads to excessive wordiness and forces them to rely upon memory to cover the agenda that requires attention. When we rely exclusively upon memory, we almost always forget at least "one little thing," which requires we waste our time by making a call-back. I am fond of the line spoken by George C. Scott as the protagonist in the film *Patton:* "I don't believe in paying for the same piece of real estate twice!" This relates directly to the need to organize our calls to avoid unnecessary duplication of effort and accompanying losses of time. Outlines also help us to sound more credible and persuasive.

As you will see from the form on page 9, my outline format provides space for noting practically everything that is going to be covered during a call, from the statements I need to make to the questions I require answers for to the notes of what is said during the call by both parties. I have also written down the name of the person I am

Telephone Notation Format

<table>
<tr><td colspan="2">NAME ORGANIZATION DATE PHONE PAGE 1</td></tr>
<tr><td>Statements: 1.
2.</td><td>Questions: 1.
2.</td></tr>
<tr><td>FLOW SHEET

"PERSONALISMS"
(are put in quotation marks)</td><td>NEW QUESTIONS AS
THEY ARISE
IN THE CONVERSATION</td></tr>
</table>

calling, his or her company and phone number, and the date; and the page number of the notes is indicated in the upper right-hand corner.

From the time I have dialed your number, I am ready to write down everything that is being said in key-word notes, as a debater or an attorney in a courtroom would. I make my notes in the lower left-hand portion of the page. It really does not matter what is being said in regard to the subject matter at the beginning of the call. I will be recording everything.

For instance, let's say that I called you about a forthcoming seminar that your company was going to sponsor. At first, I asked you, "How is the weather in Cincinnati today?" You responded by saying that it was cloudy and it "looks like rain." I will be listening to what you are saying and condensing your speech into key words such as "cloudy/maybe rain." Why am I recording seemingly irrelevant details such as these? I am in no position during the call to judge the merits or later significance of what you are saying at that point. The fact that rain is expected may inform whether I suggest we postpone our plans or whether I pack my trench coat for the trip. In short, this little detail may prove to be very significant at a later date.

The outline also provides for what I term "personalisms." These are distinctive phrases or words that the other person utters during the call, which I may wish to use either during the call or at a later date to create a bond with the person. Sometimes by echoing "pet words" back to another person we can create a greater sense of affiliation with that person.

Once when I was negotiating with an organization at long distance, my contact mentioned that if one of our programs attracted a certain number of participants, there would be a "spiff" in the deal for me. Immediately, I wrote down that term and put it in quotation marks on my outline, earmarking it as a personalism. A spiff, by the way, is an extra monetary incentive. I thought it was a rather distinctive term because I had never heard it from a representative of the industry with which I was working. This notation was to become very significant.

After a few weeks, my contract with the organization came in the mail without any mention of the spiff. I telephoned my contact and mentioned this to him, making a point of using his term. I said, "I distinctly remember you said something about a spiff." He remembered our agreement immediately and promised to send me a revised contract. I do not think his memory would have been as vivid if I had not offered *his precise term back to him.*

Handling Spontaneous Questions

Quite often we will be talking on the phone and a significant question will pop into mind about a subject only remotely connected to what is being discussed at that moment. Rather than blurting it out, or worse, forgetting about it altogether, which normally occurs without a notation system, I either place a question mark in the lower right-hand column of the outline page or write a brief key-word note in that spot to remind myself that there is a new subject area that requires attention before the call concludes.

As I cover the statements I wished to make, as set forth on the outline before the call, I will cross out the questions or statements as they are covered and recorded in the form of key-word notes. Usually, at the end of a call, I will have an opportunity to review the outline to determine if any significant areas have not been covered to that point. If so, they can then be brought up in a smooth fashion.

Signposting: Tell Them Where You're Going

Using your outline format, one of the most effective ways to manage time over the phone is to set the tone of the call right away by announcing your agenda. This is advantageous because it alerts the other party to the fact that there is a limited number of issues or areas you intend to cover. It also helps you to avoid irrelevant dialogue. Such an opener can be phrased as follows:

> *"Hello, Bill? This is Gary Goodman in Glendale. How are you today? Good.*
>
> *The reason I'm calling is in respect to three things I'd like to cover with you, okay?"*

Immediately, Bill is alerted that I have explicit objectives for our call, and I enlist his cooperation in making the call successful by using the simple request "okay?" before proceeding.

Who Cares about the Weather? Handling Small Talk

There are two distinct points of view in regard to the value of small talk, or brief exchanges about the weather, "How are you doing?" and the like. One view is that such talk is a waste of time and deserves no place in business communications. The other perspective is that small talk serves as a social lubricant, making it easier for parties to proceed to the mechanics of the matter at hand.

I once subscribed to the "time wasting" school of thought before I had the opportunity of being exposed to those who were very successful employing such "icebreakers," especially with people with whom they had not previously spoken. I find a brief exchange of pleasantries at the beginning of a call does more good, generally, than harm. It frequently sets a "warmer" tone for the call, which actually *saves time in the long run.*

As is mentioned in Chapter 3, there are significant regional differences in telephone communication in the United States, with which we need to be familiar. Very often those in the South are comfortable exchanging good tidings and personalized greetings, whereas many folks in the East "don't have time for that stuff." We need to be prepared to use those techniques that are fitting for particular regions.

"Sorry, but You Reached Me at a Bad Time"

Are there really better times than others during which to conduct business by telephone? I have asked this question of hundreds of people, and the answer is a resounding yes.

Numbers of studies in recent years point out that there seem to be peak performance cycles during the business day. It is generally held that it is better to reach people during an "up" energy cycle than during a "downswing." When do these periods occur? The peak of our energy and effectiveness comes at around 10:00 to 11:30 A.M., and our most pronounced "low" occurs after 2:30 P.M., when our lunch and our weary bones beg us for rest.

Telephone activity, according to one study, seems to follow this pattern. Calls from business telephones seemed to "peak around 11 A.M., drop off to only about half that peak volume between noon and 1 P.M., then rise to a secondary peak, not quite so high as the morning totals, around 3 P.M."[3]

As this chapter is being written, evidence is being advanced that there may be other physiological patterns and preferred activity periods among different people. Some folks are supposedly "larks," ready to perform at 100 percent early in the morning, whereas other "owls" do not really come alive until after 2:30 in the afternoon.

These general trends and preferences cannot predict how a particular person will react to a given call, about a specific matter, on one day or the next.

It Sometimes Pays to Do Things Differently

Clever telephone communicators who wish to reach otherwise inaccessible executives and clients will often play by different rules. Instead of calling their quarry during peak times, they will go against accepted wisdom and place their call very early in the morning. The reasoning is simple. Bosses and executives, being busy and hard-working types, hate to waste time being stuck in morning traffic jams. By arriving at the office one or two hours early, they can get a jump on their day in a relatively calm environment. They can also check up on those who are late.

Very often, when savvy telephone communicators call this early in the morning, they find the executive answers his or her phone personally, without an intermediary screening the call. The same logic and good fortune may apply to placing the call very late in the afternoon. Frequently, the only person who is present, and who cares about answering the night line, will be the boss.

When you are in doubt as to the best time to reach someone with whom you expect to have telephonic dealings, either ask the party when a call would be convenient or inquire about this subject with someone who might know the party's peak work periods and times of relative availability.

Setting Telephone Appointments and Teleconferencing

With the pace of business activity seeming to get more hectic all the time, we could use a format through which we might accomplish more with each telephone call while reducing the number of wasteful face-to-face meetings we have with business contacts. One of the best means to accomplish this goal, and save plenty of time, is through the proper use of the *telephone appointment* or *telephone conference.*

Not long ago, I was having a typical telephone call with a business prospect. Having advanced the idea of doing business with each other, my counterpart, Woody, suggested we get together for lunch somewhere near his office. Instead of seizing the opportunity, as I had done several times in the past, I attempted something moderately risky.

I knew if I traveled to meet Woody, it would kill at least one-half day commuting on the freeways in Los Angeles. I also recognized that historically very little of a significant nature has been accomplished in respect to "detail work" over cocktails. We would probably spend the better part of an entire day dealing with extraneous matters, while the productive work time might amount to only twenty or thirty minutes of focused discussion. Recognizing these drawbacks, I said: "Woody, I'd like to have lunch with you, and let's plan on it after we get the wheels turning with this program. In the meantime, let's see how much we can accomplish by phone and mail, okay?"

Woody seemed a little surprised by the suggestion, but readily complied. As it turns out, that particular luncheon was completely unnecessary, as we accomplished our planning primarily by telephone and mail. In essence, what we did was set up a series of brief *telephone meetings,* which were focused on specific agendas, as would be face-to-face interactions. We would agree in advance to specific times at which one of us would call the other, and both of us would be prepared to cover certain specified areas.

It is important to point out that these telephone appointments were set up in *the same formal spirit as are other appointments.* When they are set up, each party is notified of the specific date and time, and such information is recorded on the respective calendars of the parties.

Both persons are agreeing to be in specific places at a specific time for a probable span of time. Etiquette suggests that changes in telephone appointments and cancellations be announced to the other person as expediently as possible.

If you are operating through intermediaries, as you are when pursuing a busy executive through his or her secretary, the telephone appointment may be the best way of securing the attention of the executive for a discussion. By alerting the secretary to your proposed agenda, the time it will take to cover the subjects, and your available telephone meeting times, you will often be granted an "electronic audience" with the person, where it might be remotely possible to have him or her set aside an entire "appointment slot" for your personal visit.

Teleconferencing is presently used by numbers of organizations that appreciate the timesaving value of the telephone. Most teleconferencing is accomplished by linking two or more locations together during a particular call. For example, executives with branches of a company in Detroit, Los Angeles, and Cleveland would participate in the same call, as any two locations might, during ordinary transmissions. The key here is that the people involved are simulating a meeting without having to go to the expense of having a face-to-face get-together.

Unlike "personal" meetings, however, the teleconference loses much in nonverbal texture and can be a much less rich and relaxed format through which to interact. Rather than being in a situation where participants may "jump in" after receiving nonverbal encouragement, speakers in a teleconference usually need to be formally acknowledged before gaining the floor. Accordingly, when several people speak at the same time, the communication channel is overloaded, allowing listeners little chance of hearing any message with clarity.

One of my clients in the airline industry uses teleconferencing with very positive results. The company has regularly scheduled Monday morning sales meetings where as many as seven or eight stations will participate. Each station or terminal manager will discuss his or her sales performance over the last week, with the vice-president of sales moderating the meeting. All managers are free to ask questions and make comments if they wish, after hearing a formal report. This format encourages cooperation, and the "public" nature of the conference call fosters interstation rivalry and competition, which contribute to better performance.

Commonsense Remedies

A number of timesaving suggestions are, of course, matters of common sense. One "timeless" suggestion is to call ahead before embarking for an appointment to make sure that your party will be there when you arrive.

My wife and I decided to visit the "family cabin" for a quiet weekend of relaxation and reading. It had been about a year since we made such a trek, and we were sure we would find the place full of cobwebs and in various ways in disrepair. Before we hopped in the car for the two-hour trip, my wife decided to call one of our relatives to find out if the water needed to be turned on. We already had a key, so this was the only detail in question. Or so we thought.

My wife, remembering that from time to time the family would rent out the cabin, decided to ask if it was vacant. The response was that the place had been "rented for months." We were much happier hearing this bad news from a friendly relative than we would have been hearing it from an unhappy "squatter," if we had not made the call before traveling.

Take Charge!

There is a sense of urgency about hearing a telephone ring unlike hearing just about any other sound. We are compelled to answer. Have you ever noticed how rapidly someone with whom you are speaking in person will reach out and grab an incoming call? Almost without exception, the incoming call takes priority, irrespective of its significance. It is truly the "brave tele-time manager" who can shut out incoming telephone calls when other tasks require his or her attention. This rare ability is very much worth cultivating.

Each of us needs to recognize his or her own personal "style" in respect to handling our telephone time. Some folks find they are comfortable juggling several calls at once, on numbers of lines. Others find that giving their complete attention to one call at a time is more comfortable and productive. I find myself in the second camp.

I often suggest that executives set aside certain "open times" during business days for speaking to incoming callers. This is in the same spirit as companies that post certain times during which "salesmen are seen." By limiting the open times the executive is not only alerting the world that there are good and bad times during which he or she may be reached but is also making the caller more efficient in his or her pursuit. The executive is, in effect, saying: "You will have a much greater chance of speaking to me if you will call between 7:30 and 9:30 A.M."

The same principle applies to making outgoing calls for the purpose of either initiating a contact or calling someone back. I find that it is easier to make a series of calls during a given time period than staggering the calls throughout a longer period of time or over a complete day. A certain "irresistible momentum" is building from one call to the next when we make a number of calls in rapid order. For this reason, I like to set aside blocks of time during which I place the majority of my calls during the day. The rest of the day consists of receiving calls and performing other activities.

Remembering Our ABC's

A well-regarded method of managing time is the suggestion that we make lists of those activities of greatest importance to us at a given time, and call this our *"A" list.* Those tasks that are less important, yet are worth doing, are placed on a *"B" list.* Finally, we have our *"C" list,* or collection of tasks of least importance to us at a given time.

There is no reason why this method cannot be adapted for telephonic use. Certainly, we have calls to make and receive that can be placed into one of the three priority groupings. When time becomes particularly tight, focusing upon the *A*'s is appropriate, and as time becomes a bit more loose, we can work our way through the *B*'s and *C*'s.

I have found that the best time to plan our calls is the evening before we intend to make them. In this way, we can develop a broad overview of what we hope to accomplish by phone while getting a start on actual call planning through use of the outline format set forth in this chapter. Moreover, we will be able to better integrate telephone communication into our overall business design, assuring that we make the most of our time on and off the telephone.

Notes

1. Alan H. Wurtzel and Colin Turner, "Latent Functions of the Telephone: What Missing the Extension Means," in *The Social Impact of the Telephone,* Ithiel de Sola Pool, ed. (Cambridge, Mass.: The MIT Press, 1977), p. 251.

2. Alvin Toffler, *The Third Wave* (New York: Bantam Books, 1981), pp. 194–207.

3. Martin Mayer, "The Telephone and the Uses of Time," in *The Social Impact of the Telephone,* p. 234.

2

Developing the Telephone Ear: Listening Problems, Opportunities, and Tips

If there is any one secret of success it lies in the ability to get the other person's point of view and see things from his angle as well as your own.—Henry Ford

When I was growing up, I knew a boy named Joey who was the proverbial class clown. It seemed that everything he did was foolish or designed to make the rest of us laugh, teachers excluded. I suppose Joey was a lot of trouble, though he certainly could deflate adult puffery in imaginative ways.

One of the most common refrains that students heard in those days was "Joey, you're not *listening!*" He was usually planning the next prank or was too busy engaged in a present one to dutifully follow Teacher's "lesson plan." We all wondered what would happen to Joey and his case of terminal "tune-out." We figured he'd become a comedian or wind up in jail. Either way, nobody would be able to wipe off that devilish grin from his face. Or so we thought.

For about a week and a half, Joey did not come to school. The tragic story finally reached the playground. Joey's dad had been hit by a car in full view of his young son. When Joey did return to school, he was a changed person. Nobody had to chide him for not listening anymore. Apparently, he sensed he was the "head of his family" and had to use his time wisely. He had to look out for himself. He had become a very *motivated listener.*

I saw Joey a few years after high school. On a grocery clerk's pay, he was putting himself through college at night while supporting his family of four. It was ironic that he took on more responsibility than his classmates did at that early point in their adult lives. I remember thinking that he had created a lot of work for himself at that time in his life. Another two years passed, and Joey said he was finishing his studies to become a CPA. He was obviously happy. He seemed more settled than I and most of our old friends. Who would have predicted that our class clown would become so "respectable" and such a serious achiever?

His story is not unusual in respect to "listening behavior." Though many of us are not obstructionists in any way, we are not motivated listeners, either. Major events do not occur to most of us, catalyzing instant and dramatic change in listening behavior. We tend to "drone on" with the same level of listening skill, or we become gradually deskilled, whereby our listening habits get worse.

Most of Us Are Poor Listeners!

It is a fact that if the failure to listen could be called a disease, we would be facing an epidemic in this country right at this moment. Most folks are dismal listeners.

According to research, we only listen with 25 to 50 percent efficiency. This means that 50 to 75 percent of the messages to which we are exposed are not processed consciously. They simply *zip* right by us!

How did we get this way? What are the challenges we face in listening? How can we become better listeners both on and off the telephone?

Inadequate Training

Most high schools and colleges offer communication courses of several varieties, including competitive speech events. These worthwhile activities place emphasis upon self-expression and improvement of delivery, among other skills. Until recently, however, there have been few, if any, courses devoted to helping people to learn the art of listening, which is so critical for producing effective and successful communication between people. I would venture to say that it is the unusually progressive elementary school that devotes any resources to this area. Is it really any wonder that people are unskilled?

Listening Fictions

Before we can really sense the right path for listening improvement, we need to clear away obstacles to understanding. These come in the form of fictions that we believe about listening.

1. "If you have 'two good ears,' listening will happen automatically."

Unfortunately, there is little that is "automatic" about the listening process. Listening, in other words, takes *effort.* Unless we are really prepared to listen, we are unlikely to perform this activity competently.

2. "Listening and hearing are really the same things."

Most researchers distinguish these activities by pointing out that "hearing" is merely perceiving sounds, whereas listening is the process of making sense of the sounds we hear. One activity is passive; the other requires *action* on our part.

3. "Listening to another person is an unselfish act, in which we are giving of ourselves."

This statement is partially true and partially false. It is true that we use listening as a "gift" we give to other people, especially when they come to us for the purpose of "crying on our shoulders." In fact, through listening we can engage in a process that others find extremely supportive and satisfying.

At the same time, few "gifts" are given without charge of some sort. One of the best reasons to listen is that if we do, we will be held in higher regard by those with whom we interact. Moreover, we will be exposed to opportunities and valuable information in this fashion. We should listen, in other words, because *it is a practical means for accomplishing our goals through other people.*

4. "Listeners are born, not made."

Listening effectively, like speaking effectively, is a learned activity. When we are born, we don't know the language that we will have to speak to belong to our culture. Just as language is learned, we learn to "listen for" certain sounds and meanings and to discount others.

5. "I will be more effective with people by being a better speaker rather than a better listener."

One of the best ways to "sell" somebody an idea is to help the person to "sell herself." This is acknowledged by some of the best "persuaders" in industry. We tend to think, however, that persuasion works best when one person is flapping his/her jaws at another while issuing forth a profusion of ten-dollar words. People sell themselves by answering our questions and by volunteering information on their own. If we do not provide them with the "space" in which to express their ideas, they will not become committed to a course of action with the same sort of "ownership" that they may otherwise.

Ideally, of course, the good telephone communicator will cultivate skills in listening *and* speaking. In becoming better listeners, we *should become better speakers as well.* By listening we can gain insight into the other person's point of view and efficiently gear our message to his or her personal situation. This saves a lot of time because we are not "shotgunning" our messages, but taking calm, accurate aim at a known target.

6. "It is the responsibility of the speaker *to make me want to listen to what he or she is saying!"*

"He's so *dull!*" We've heard this statement many times, and perhaps we've said it ourselves. There is no question that some speakers are difficult to listen to because they speak too slowly or in monotone or because their treatment of a subject is uninspired. It is also true that the great majority of speakers are lackluster in their performance skill. This deficiency is compounded on the telephone because many speakers are even less diligent when using this medium.

This presents problems for listeners. It is clearly easier to "tune out" a dull speaker than a dynamic one. We need to remember, however, that effective listening is the responsibility of the *listener more than the speaker.* Chances are the dull speaker is doing the best he or she can, but, as listeners, we can note the poor delivery of the speaker and compensate for this problem by "embellishing" the message as we process it. In short, *we* can make a message more interesting by allowing our imaginations to work for us.

> 7. *"Listening isn't nearly as interesting or as rewarding as speaking."*

We take pride in our speaking abilities. We tend to admire quipsters and punsters and those who either have fun using language or are particularly eloquent. In fact, on some occasions we give awards, medals, and plaques to public speakers and "communicators." To my knowledge we rarely give anyone a decoration for being a great listener. As a result, we tend to hold listening in lower regard than speaking and perceive this activity as less enjoyable.

Trained listeners can tell you that they are having a grand time when they "do their thing." Many will say that it is exhilarating to develop an accurate understanding of another person's point of view. To really "see the world" from another person's vantage point is a rare and exciting event. It is not too much unlike the thrill actors experience when they feel, for the first time, what it is like to "stand in the shoes" of another character. This sort of identification with another person creates closeness with them, as well as increased understanding of ourselves and our own worlds.

It is also rewarding to help another person express something difficult by providing a supportive atmosphere for their comments and ideas. Some television interviewers owe their effectiveness at "bringing someone out" to their sensitive and refined skills in listening.

> 8. *"I will impress people more by dazzling them with diction than by listening."*

Our success with others is clearly tied into the extent to which we can impress them. When we undertake the process of making ourselves impressive to another person, we tend to think in terms of *what we are going to say*. We might even rehearse a few great lines to spring on them at our first opportunity. Seldom, though, does the situation conspire with us to afford an opportunity to utter those "golden words."

Think of people with whom you enjoy spending time. They probably make you feel important and worthwhile. Chances are pretty good that they validate you by listening to what you have to say. When we encounter people who are truly good listeners, they make a lasting impression upon us. We tend to attribute to them higher intelligence, among other desirable traits. (Think about it. Only the most *intelligent* folks would have the good sense to listen to *our* ideas!)

As a consultant, I get a good amount of my business over the phone. Numbers of folks call me to find out more about in-house training and upcoming seminars. I know they are having two conversations at the same time when they get me on the line. Conversation 1 is devoted to talking with me. Conversation 2 is the one they are having with themselves. They are evaluating my responses as they hear them, while asking themselves, "Does he *really* sound like a telephone communication expert?" My mission, in part, is to reassure them that, indeed, I am a phone professional. How do I achieve this? By listening I have found that I impress my clients more than by dazzling them with the latest findings from behavioral research in some obscure corner of the business communication field. Many "experts" feel they need to impress others by telling them things. I have found that asking intelligent questions, listening to the responses, and building a reciprocal relationship on the phone makes me much more impressive.

9. "Frankly, some subjects bore me to tears, and no matter what I do, I cannot help falling asleep when I hear them."

Public-speaking teachers are fond of a line: "There are no boring subjects; only boring speakers." There is some wisdom in the thought that speakers should do their best to keep their listeners interested in what they are saying, through more effective treatment and delivery of subject matter. Failing this, it is up to listeners to *make the subject interesting to themselves.* How may we do this?

I have found that it is relatively easy to dissociate ourselves from subjects and adopt an attitude of "This doesn't really relate to me." We might even be accurate, in a sense, as the subject may seem to us to be "coming from left field." It is a little more difficult to *make a subject we are hearing relate to ourselves.*

If we have to listen to a speaker on the phone or off, we should get the most out of the occasion as possible. To do this, we should constantly try to relate what we are hearing to *our actual or probable experience.* We should ask ourselves, "How *might* this information be valuable to me, now or in the future?" By answering this question we will find an experiential "hook" upon which we can place the information to which we are exposed. It will be surprising to note how one's experience grows as a result of this sort of "stretching exercise."

10. "I always get distracted when I'm on the phone. It's harder to listen on the phone than in person."

If you find other people are constantly putting things in front of you to sign when you are on a call, or they are trying to ask you questions or get your attention, you do face an obstacle to effective listening. It is up to you, though, to stop this behavior by letting it be known that your telephone communications are no less important than the matters being thrust into your lap by face-to-face interlopers. By allowing distractions we perpetuate them.

Listening on the phone is *different from, but not necessarily inferior to, listening in the physical presence of another person.* It is true that we don't have the kinds of visual cues that can help us to understand the message and find it more interesting, as the use of gestures allows. Nonetheless, when we are on the phone, we are beyond the reach of *distracting* gestures, physical surroundings, clothing, facial expressions, and other phenomena that can cause us to lose track of the message.

Negative Listening Habits: "Am I a Poor Telephone Listener?"

There are numbers of counterproductive listening styles. Here is a partial list of problem listeners.

The Selective Listener

The selective listener is one *who hears remarks only of obvious interest to him or her and filters out those messages that are not of instant relevance.* We can tell when we have selective listeners on the phone when they give exuberant feedback at one stage of the call, especially when we are speaking about a subject "near and dear" to them. They can next be heard "fading away" as the subject moves to an area outside of their "pet area." They may give us halfhearted grunts and "uh-huhs," but we know we do not have their total attention.

To an extent, selective listening is normal. We do tend to tune in to information that seems to be timely for ourselves and our immediate concerns. It becomes a problem when it gets excessive. What can we do when we recognize we have a selective listener on the line? How can we keep him or her from tuning out and fading away?

What we need to do to keep the interest of the selective listener is to make the subject we are discussing seem to be of immediate relevance to that person. Surely you have used the techniques I am going to suggest without having thought consciously about your strategy. In fact, you might be able to tell me more about this technique than I can tell you. You'll really appreciate the technique when it is revealed to you, no doubt.

What word have I used significantly more than any other within the last three sentences? That's right, I used the word *YOU. This is one of the sweetest words in the world to a selective listener. You, you, you, you, you. The listener hears ME, ME, ME, ME, ME! This provides the sort of relevance that the selective listener craves.*

Another technique is to use the other person's name frequently. "And, Bill, the next thing I thought was how lucky I was." People love to hear their names played back to them. An easy approach is to modulate your voice in such a way as to make it more compelling. This may be accomplished by either lowering the voice suddenly or raising it. Both nuances "snap" the listener into a more attentive mode.

The last resort is to turn control of the conversation over to the selective listener. He or she will use the opportunity to wax at great length about his tennis game, or entertain you with vignettes from the family outing at the cabin last summer. You should specifically avoid open-ended questions that allow the person to emote about what he or she "feels" about the matter.

The Insulated Listener

The insulated listener is the person who hears only those messages that are pleasant, while blocking out messages that are negative or unpleasant. Bosses tend to be insulated listeners, or so they seem from my experience. They want to hear "the good word," but turn a deaf ear to the response that there isn't any at the moment. The problem with insulated listeners is that they are shielding themselves from a certain amount of reality that will probably rear its head and lash out in fury for having been ignored. How might we effectively deal with the insulated listener?

Some folks suggest we play "bad news/good news." Here's how it works. We tell the boss we have bad news. We spit it out and quickly indicate that there is a more pleasant side to the story. I find this approach problematic because, by definition, the insulated listener is going to tune us out when hearing that bad news is forthcoming.

Another approach is the "good news/bad news" thrust. Here we start out by bringing our listener to the summit of good feeling by imparting a positive tale. Next we will "shaft" the person to the lowest valley with the bad news. I suspect the "distance" between the pinnacle and the pit is too great. The negative news may seem too stark at that point.

I like to combine these methods with what has been called the "sandwich technique." We sandwich the negative news between two pieces of positive news.

"Bill, we think you are doing a fine job here at Abba Zappa Pump Company. If, however, you could come in from 8:30 to 5:30 like the rest of us, we think you'd get a good deal more accomplished. In doing so, you will be able to really show your abilities and move forward!" This approach takes the sting out of the bad news by leaving the call or statement on a positive note.

The Defensive Listener

The defensive listener takes practically everything someone else says as a personal attack. The defensive listener's problem is spending the great majority of time available in a situation defending a bruised ego rather than dealing with the matter at hand.

Several messages cause defensiveness in our listeners. Some of these messages are: evaluation, control, strategy, neutrality, superiority, and certainty. We will examine each kind of message in Chapter 4 when we speak about handling conflict on the phone. We will note that the best way of dealing with a defensive listener is to employ a supportive message strategy that gradually brings the person out of a threatened frame of mind.

The Ambusher

The ambusher is the listener who cannot wait to jump into the conversation to disagree with us. Something we said must have disturbed this person because all he or she can do is rehearse "brilliant" counterattacks while impatiently waiting to seize the communication channel. One of the signs of the ambusher is feedback that seems "hollow," nonexistent, or outright negative while we are speaking. We can sense that the person is waiting to "zing" us with an argumentative arrow that is eagerly awaiting release from a quivering bow. What can we do if we think our listener is on military maneuvers while we are speaking?

I have found that a direct approach is effective. I interrupt myself in the middle of an idea and ask: "Is there anything *questionable* about what I am covering, or do you have any questions at this point?" Note what we do with this kind of question. By using the word "questionable" I am intentionally employing a negative term. If there is negativity, I want to deal with it *now,* so my listener may go back to the urgent business of listening. After I use this term, I give my listener another option. I ask if there are "any questions." This phrase is usually perceived as neutral or positive. If I misdiagnosed my listener's problem, and he wasn't going to ambush me after all, he will simply say, "No, I don't have any questions." He will not even hear the negative term "questionable." I can then continue speaking with confidence.

The Insensitive Listener

The insensitive listener takes everything he or she hears literally and ignores the tone of voice used by the speaker. The problem with insensitive listeners is that they are missing a great deal by concentrating only upon content while not paying attention to the "emotional agenda" that may accompany it.

I suggest to clients the idea of adding a provision on most telephone message pads. Pads should not only allow space for noting the name, phone number, time of call, and brief message, as they commonly do, but should also leave a line for *tone of voice of the caller.*

This would accomplish a few things. It would alert the receiver of the call that tone of voice is a significant area of interest and should be noted. This information may be extremely pertinent and valuable as well. If your office negotiates contracts, as many do, it is useful and highly advantageous to have a feeling for the mood of the prospective client before we speak with him or her on the phone. If the client sounds friendly, this may indicate we have more latitude than if the tone sounds worried or slightly negative.

It also makes good sense to have an accurate idea of "where someone is coming from" emotionally as we speak with him or her on the phone. When we have such an idea, we may better identify with the person and impart the feeling that we are treating him/her as an individual.

Faulty Listening Responses

Many of us tend to employ faulty listening responses when we speak with another person on the phone. These habits should be examined and overcome in order to increase our skills.

Dismissing the Message Too Quickly

A common habit among poor listeners is to prematurely dismiss the importance or accuracy of a message known to come from a given speaker. "He never knows that he is talking about," we may think. As a result of this kind of judgment, we tune out and frequently miss information that could be of value to us. I am fond of the slightly facetious line "Even a broken clock is accurate at least two times a day!" This statement reminds us that we may learn something or hear something accurately from a source in whom we invest little confidence.

We may choose to dismiss the message because there are numbers of technical terms being spoken that are taxing for us to decode. On the other hand, we might tell ourselves that the information is "too elementary" for someone of our "stature." Many folks conclude that there won't be "anything new" in what they are going to hear, so they may just as well tune out and save some energy. "This is going to be *so* dull" is another self-statement that encourages us to become, as one acquaintance put it, "a space case."

"I Can't Stand This Speaker!"

When we have negatively judged the speaker, it is easy to criticize him or her instead of listening to the message. We may choose to concentrate our negative judgments upon voice, organization of ideas, or general "approach" to the conversation.

This sort of criticism may be a signal that we are "defensive" about the speaker, subject, or occasion for the call. By asking ourselves, "What could be threatening me about this call?" we may gain insight as well as permit ourselves to return to constructive listening and understanding.

Responding to "Red Flag" Words

"Red flags" are words and phrases that evoke an almost immediate emotional response in us. Often this response is negative, as when some of us are exposed to "four-letter words." When we hear a red flag term, our attention shifts immediately from a perception of the overall subject to the rightness and wrongness of the use of the term.

Red flags throw us off the track and make listening difficult. We need to identify our own "problem words" and recognize that a speaker's use of them is usually not designed to evoke our wrath or distract us. Knowing this, we may be better able to resist the distracting allure of these terms.

For some folks a red flag may be merely a mispronounced word. They think, "This speaker is *wrong* in her use of that term. I *know* it! Could *I* be wrong? Let me think. . . ." This journey into "meanings" can last a long time, preventing the listener from hearing important information.

Daydreaming

People are capable of thinking at an extremely fast speed. It is said that we can "process" or hear as many as 600 to 650 words per minute with excellent comprehension. Most speakers, however, speak at a rate of 100 to 150 words per minute when they are chatting in person, and some speak even more slowly on the phone. This gap between listening capability and verbal delivery speeds contributes to daydreaming because listeners are "ahead" of speakers.

Listeners should be aware of this built-in perceptual tendency to wander, and compensate for it by using thought speed to help the speaker to make or support her point, or to constructively "guess" where the speaker is headed and "check up" on the accuracy of this hunch. These sorts of "games" played by a listener may contribute to the overall success of a message and phone call while harnessing what could otherwise be nonconstructive energy.

Failure to React to the Speaker

Some folks give incomplete or little feedback to a speaker when they are listening. Instead of telling the person we are alive, well, and understanding the message, the speaker is left without any clue as to our level of understanding, agreement, or support for the message. Lack of feedback causes communication problems.

As speakers, especially on the phone, we need to know "how our message is doing" with the listener. If we have no idea, we will tend to become more gingerly in our expressions, hoping not to offend the person, or we may say the same thing three or four different ways to make sure he or she gets the point. Without continuous feedback, though, we will not be clear as to the effect our message is having, which will cause us to become inefficient communicators.

Listeners can help out by periodically issuing some sounds such as "uh-huh" and "yes." These and other signs of listening will be perceived by the speaker as supportive.

Avoiding Difficult Material

"This is much too complex a subject for me" is a line that many listeners tell themselves when they believe they are going to be asked to listen to technical or involved information. They have prejudged the difficulty of the material and cause themselves to be "inept" at handling it. This keeps people from growing and expanding their capabilities.

Sometimes receptionists and secretaries will use this kind of judgment as a "cop-out" so they will not have to bother handling a lengthy or difficult phone message. They shuffle the call to someone else who grits his teeth over the "difficulty" of the information being transmitted!

Physical Unpreparedness

An amazing number of telephone communicators answer calls without having the appropriate recording tools, appointment books, and other relevant business devices at their immediate disposal. Moreover, the "files" or computer access codes needed for summoning relevant information are often "away from our desks" when we most need them.

We are also unprepared in a strict *physical* sense. As schoolteachers were fond of pointing out, posture is related to performance. If we tend to become supine, or "reclined" at our desks as the day wears on, our telephone personalities will tend to come across as lethargic and disinterested.

Stereotypical Listening

"That call is from *Canada?* It must be ______!" This sort of expression is frequently made by folks who respond to stereotyped images of other people and companies.

I know a number of business people who are so enamored with "bigness" that when they hear a name of a corporate giant, such as IBM or Xerox, they almost fall to their knees right away and worship the name. Anything attributed to such organizations is considered "good." This kind of uncritical acceptance of references to organizations reflects stereotypical thinking as much as prejudiced views about folks who are calling from different regions of the country. In both cases we have made a prejudgment, which is followed by fitting all we hear into the mold. After making this judgment, we will tend to perceive only that information consistent with the preconception while filtering out contrary information.

Understanding Your Listening Style

One of the first steps in becoming a better listener is to understand our listening style. There are four basic modes in which we listen: pleasurable, discriminative, critical, and empathic. Each mode is appropriate for processing certain information, and inappropriate for other sorts of data.

Pleasurable listening has "enjoyment" as its aim. This is the mode in which many of us watch entertainment shows on television. We are looking to laugh or to be diverted from the serious concerns of business or family. As a result, when our favorite television comedy show tries to "preach to us" or "educate us," we sometimes feel our communication contract with the program has been breached.

Discriminative listening is geared to receiving facts and ideas while promoting understanding. Our business hours are often spent in this listening mode. When information is presented to us in a logical and straightforward fashion, discriminative listening is facilitated. When we find ourselves listening in this way, it is particularly frustrating to deal with folks who are disorganized, vague, or verbose.

Critical listening is used to discern whether a speaker is using information in an appropriate fashion. For instance, we listen critically to those who wish to persuade us to buy something or to change our attitudes about an important subject. This kind of self-protective listening is extremely important in a society such as ours, where the "marketplace of ideas" can offer us absurd and possibly dangerous notions to which we are asked to subscribe. When we listen critically, we are attempting to analyze the logic and reasonableness of the speaker's propositions while listening "between the lines" for overly broad assumptions or conveniently "missing" facts.

Empathic listening is aimed at becoming sensitive to the point of view and feelings of another person. When we serve as a "sounding board" or a "shoulder to cry on," we are serving an empathic listening function. Many times our clients and associates call upon us to be empathic listeners. We need to recognize that their request is to be "heard" and not to be evaluated or criticized. This sort of listening has what might be called a soothing or therapeutic value for the speaker.

It is important that we recognize: (1) our tendency to listen in one characteristic mode or other and (2) the desirability of switching modes to suit the speaker, subject, and occasion. We have all run across folks who are stuck in one mode or other. There is the person who is a "critical listener" in all situations, including inappropriate ones. He or she joins us on a tour of a city, and instead of *appreciating* the description of the sights provided by the tour guide, insists that some information must have been left out. Other folks seem to be forever trapped in an appreciative mode and speak about how beautiful a telephone communicator's voice is, while not listening to the content that the voice is trying to convey.

Tips for Developing Your "Telephone Ear"

There are several practices that can enhance our listening powers. We should state one thing as we consider these suggestions. It will be impossible to incorporate all of the recommended changes at once. Work on them gradually, trying to incorporate more over time. This will be more realistic for you and will contribute to more lasting change.

1. *Get more involved by asking questions.* Many of us are too passive when we listen to others on the phone. Try to generate intelligent questions, which will tell the speaker you are following the flow of ideas and are interested in the topic.
2. *Don't allow emotional words to throw you off the track.* Try to identify on a piece of paper those words or terms that really "offend" you or tend to make you daydream. After writing them down, make a deal with yourself that you will make an extra effort in the future to not let these terms and phrases distract you. Be especially aware of "happy words," such as "mother," "freedom," "free choice," and "nice." "Devil words," such as "criminal," "unfair," and "anti-," can also summon strong emotional reactions if we allow them to do so.
3. *Listen for an organized understanding of the message.* As noted elsewhere, speakers do not always deliver their ideas to us in neat packages with ribbons tied around them. As listeners, we need to "repackage" their ideas to make them suitable for interpretation and being remembered. Having an ongoing mental "outline" of what the speaker is saying can help us to interpret quickly while making a lasting memory "imprint."
4. *Try to relate the message you are hearing to your past experience or possible future experiences.* This procedure will create an association in your mind that will make the message vivid and more interesting.
5. *If you think you are "being sold a bill of goods," analyze the logic, evidence, and overall integrity of the message you are*

hearing. This is the place where critical listening is invaluable. You will probably find, over time, that your critical skills become increasingly honed, so you can ferret out ungrounded emotional appeals and other nonrational and unreasonable propositions being advanced by speakers. (If you are *really* interested in increasing your reasoning and interpretive skills, I suggest you consider signing up for college classes in such subjects as: "Argumentation and Debate," offered in speech and communication departments; "Logic," offered by philosophy departments; and "Sociological Analysis," offered by some social science departments. There is a great thrill in confronting unscrupulous speakers with the folly of their assertions.)

6. *Don't prepare rebuttals to the speaker's points until you have heard the entire message.* Often we think we know where a speaker is headed with an idea, and we formulate a response while the person is talking, only to find we have developed an inappropriate response and have missed the true idea that the person was trying to convey.

7. *Use your thinking speed, which exceeds the speaker's talking speed, to facilitate understanding rather than compete with it.* Because we can think at a rate of 600 to 650 words per minute while a speaker is talking at 100 to 150 words per minute, our tendency is to daydream. Instead, we should use our excess thinking speed to enhance the message by thinking ahead, analyzing logic, listening between the lines, and reviewing what we are hearing for greater retention.

8. *Work on increasing your attention span.* Some folks have attention spans shorter than those of hamsters, it seems. According to one report, the average attention span of a human being is *four seconds!* To develop powers of concentration, we should force ourselves, when we feel we are about to sail away on a daydream, to *repeat each word we hear the speaker utter, before we respond and before we think about something else.* This will compel us to "stay tuned" to what we are hearing. After a while we should build this behavior into a habit pattern, which is more self-sustaining.

9. *After a call has concluded, test your listening with a "clarity*

check." Ask yourself to repeat or condense the content of the conversation. Can you make good sense of what was said? Were you left with more questions than answers from the call? You should be able to repeat with great clarity what you heard.

10. *Keep an open mind about the speaker and message.* We should get in touch with any bad feelings we have about the person on the other end of the line, so we will not block out important information that the speaker may share with us.

11. *Be physically prepared to listen.* I mean this in two respects. First, good listening takes energy. After you have *really* listened to another person for a period of time, you will probably feel a little fatigued. Your pulse rate will be a little higher, and your respiration may be faster, too. Listening, in these respects, is like a sport. It takes its toll on us and exacts a more profound price if we are not prepared for the challenge. This is why it is important to sit up straight in our seats when we are on the phone, to facilitate the circulation of our blood and to help us stay alert. The usual tendency is for folks to become "reclined" as they chat, which obstructs effective listening. We should also be prepared in respect to the materials we will need access to during the call. We should have all writing and recording tools close by, so we don't create untimely pauses and lulis in the information flow of the call. Personally, I like to have my files and other information receptacles nearby, so I may have instant access to the data that may be helpful during a call.

12. *Fight distractions before your calls, and tolerate them during the calls.* To the extent possible, we should improve our listening environments. If we find a choice between answering a phone extension that is next to a noisy corridor or away from one, we should choose the quieter alternative. It is surprising how we tend to assimilate noises into our consciousness and forget they are possible impediments to clear communication. Newcomers may enter our office and ask how we can get along with such noise. We sometimes respond, "What noise?" Nonetheless, the distraction is probably decreasing our telephone effectiveness. If the distraction emerges during the call,

we should do our best to ignore it and concentrate on the message being transmitted.

13. *Set a short-range goal for listening.* What do you hope to accomplish on this call? What sorts of information can you derive that will enhance your understanding and expand your perspectives? We should motivate ourselves to listen by defining a target that we would like to reach with every call and with different kinds of calls.

14. *Listen for the central idea.* What is the speaker trying to say? What is the main theme that can be derived from this call?

15. *Take notes of all telephone conversations.* The Telephone Notation Format provided on page 9, provides one sort of outline formula that can help record ideas as you hear them. Although there are different note-taking styles we may use as listeners, including key-word, full-sentence, main-idea, and verbatim formats, I find the key-word format works best for telephone purposes. What I do is record in key words a "flow" of all the ideas that I hear during the call. If the other party begins the call by referring to the wonderful weather in Florida, I will be writing the words "weather—great." The next note I may write will record the fact that the other party wishes to discuss three things, and the words "three things" will be written. I do not judge the importance of what I am writing; this is reserved for later, after the call. I am simply trying to record or sketch the ideas I hear for later retrieval. If you need to record a literal message, another style would be better.

16. *Be a sensitive listener. Listen for feelings, facts, and ideas.* You might wish to ask yourself at the beginning of each call, "Where does this person seem to be coming from emotionally, at this point?" Your alertness to the emotional agenda will be rewarded, as you will be better able to understand and work with the person at that time.

17. *Use active listening by repeating to the satisfaction of the other person what you think he or she* meant *by a certain message.* Too often, we think we know what the other person really meant because we heard and understood the words used.

This is not a reliable assumption. Frequently, people say one thing and mean something else entirely. By checking our interpretation with the other person we are able to set straight any misunderstandings as they occur and before they come back to haunt us. I like the phrase "Now, just so I'm clear, I hear you saying you want X, Y, and Z. Is that right?" The other person may then respond by saying he or she *does* want X and Y, but Z "really isn't that important." This would require a change in interpretation on our part, which could be significant, depending on what Z really was. By the way, we should use this technique even if we think the other person might judge us to be "stupid." It is a lot smarter to achieve clarity from a conversation than to leave it misinformed and misdirected.

18. If the speaker isn't a dynamo, help out by making the message more interesting to yourself. It was mentioned previously that listeners are responsible for the degree to which they can find a message "interesting." I like to use my imagination to make the person on the other end of the line "come alive." I might imagine the other person's face, age, or clothes. I might also stand the person on his/her head in my imagination, and I do this to keep myself interested in listening. Feel free to do whatever works for you—and whatever is fun!

19. If you fail to hear something, ask the speaker to repeat or clarify the point. Too few of us do this. It is really a practical and simple behavior, too. If I am unclear about a point, I will ask: "Just so I'm clear, would you please repeat your last point for me? I'd appreciate that." Another way of getting clarity is to ask: "Would you expand on that last point, please? I would appreciate it." In both cases the speaker will probably help us out because we have been diplomatic in our request.

20. Set long-range objectives for upgrading your skills in listening. I am a great believer in the power of goals to direct and motivate performance. For most, listening has never been considered a significant enough area in which to assess strengths and weaknesses, and *plan* for improvement. Without adequate planning, however, we are not likely to produce long-lasting behavioral change and improvement. What can you use as goals? How can you measure the results?

Any of the tips for improvement outlined above may serve as *listening objectives.* Choose three or four areas to work on during the next few weeks. Commit yourself to changing your behavior in these ways on as many calls as possible. There are at least a few ways in which you may assess your progress.

Let's say you notice people telling you, "You're really a good listener!" This would be an obvious and rewarding measure of progress. If your comprehension seems to increase, you would be able to conclude that your listening is improving. If you find listening more interesting, your skills will be in the process of being refined.

In terms of phrasing an objective, I suggest you write it down on paper, and begin with the words "I will increase my skill in the area of . . ." Simply fill in the behavior you wish to work on after that point.

Helping Others to Listen More Effectively to Us

As speakers and communicators, we can do a few things to help others get more out of our messages. *Keeping their interest level high, through the use of a pleasant, yet dynamic voice,* is a good place to start. We should also understand the limitations of our listeners. It is hard, for instance, to listen in a discriminative mode for extended periods, without some sort of "diversion" supplied by humor, anecdotes, or other interest factors. Research tells us that listeners perk up their ears when they hear a story being told because they find such tales easy to identify with and entertaining.

We will also help others to listen more effectively to us by *organizing our ideas in a fashion that is easy to follow and helps recall.* When we speak of the "PEP Format" in the next chapter, we will point out an excellent, easy-to-follow organizational structure for our ideas. One of its strengths is its use of *repetition, which reinforces the idea in the listener's mind.*

We would also be wise to remember the many distractions and obstructions that come between speaker and listener on the phone and compensate for these occurrences in different ways. By making the same point in a few different ways, when we doubt that it was "received" intact the first time, we can give ourselves a greater assurance of being understood while helping the listener to fulfill his/her role comfortably.

We would be wise to remember that listening is not a skill such as riding a bicycle. We can "forget" how to listen by not practicing our techniques. With diligence, though, we can become much more masterful in this crucial telephone communication practice.

3

Developing Your Power Voice: Building Credibility and Persuasiveness

Do you remember the first time you heard your voice on a tape recording? Shocking, right? If you are like most of us, you probably went through a few changes as you listened to that electronic voice. "That's not me" is a frequent first reaction, followed by such claims as "My voice sounds so flat, so nasal." Perhaps you figured that the tape recorder was to blame until your friend indicated it was "one of the most sensitive around." Your last reaction was probably what psychologists call "flight behavior." You wanted to put a lot of distance between that contraption and yourself as quickly as possible.

Unfortunately, first experiences with feedback about our voices are rather uncomfortable and tend to make us shy away from further information about how we might sound to other people. This does not help us to develop our voices to their fullest, and we rarely have a base line of measurement from which we might elevate our abilities.

Did the Tape Recorder Lie, or Do I Really Sound Like That?

Speech scientists tell us that *we do not sound to others as we sound to ourselves.* When we hear our voices, it is like following a "map"; it's not the "territory" itself. Specifically what happens is pretty simple. When we speak, our voices are conducted through our jawbones and heads, and these body parts vibrate, causing our ears to "hear" a certain muffled representation of our voices. At approximately the same time, our ears receive the sound waves of our voices as they are bouncing off environmental objects, such as walls, furniture, and other people. It is these forms of feedback that give us our everyday acoustical image of how we sound. When other people hear our voices, their ears are not hearing the "simulcast" of two forms of vibration. Their jawbones and heads simply do not get in the way of their perception of our voices. They are dealing more directly with the "territory" itself.

Good Feedback Is Essential for Improvement

Many professional people and others endorse the idea of using a tape recorder on a regular basis in order to better understand how they are sounding to their prospects, clients, and associates and to build strategies for improvement. They claim there is no better teacher because the tape recorder is unbiased. It will not adorn our voices with sentimental judgments. It simply repeats "what is there."

To get the most out of such feedback, however, we need to know for what we are looking. We need a clearer definition of what contributes to vocal success on the phone.

What Endows a Person with a "Power Voice"?

When I think of a "power voice," I often think of newscaster Walter Cronkite or of Marlon Brando in the cinema version of *The Godfather*. Cronkite has that special bearing and dignity in his voice. He is also very believable. The sense many viewers get is, "If Walter says it's so, you can count on it." Brando's character spoke with self-assurance. His words were very well chosen and surprisingly simple and straightforward, but the Godfather seemed extremely intelligent and knowledgeable. What "magic" do these fellows possess?

Credibility

If we wish to sound powerful on the phone, we need to develop ways of appearing credible to others. Credibility, according to some scientists, consists of three traits: *trust, expertise,* and *dynamism.* To the extent that we can sound trustworthy, expert, and dynamic on the phone, we will be effective and powerful.

Curing Our "Split Personalities"

Before we can increase our credibility, we need to recognize that certain self-imposed obstacles get in our way. I have noticed a frequent occurrence as I enter offices for meetings. Two employees will be sitting at their desks talking, which is common. One will be telling the other a story, and his/her voice will be very fluid and animated, which adds interest to the story. All of a sudden, the phone rings, and what was, a moment before, a very lively person becomes another "personality" as he or she answers the phone. The phone voice is flat, lifeless, and not animated in the least. The phone call ends, and our friend once again becomes the lively storytelling personality as he or she says, "Let's see, where was I . . .?"

I suspect we have come to believe that there should be a "business voice" as opposed to a "personal voice." The business voice is to be used for business transactions, and the personal voice is to be kept under lock and key during the hours of nine to five. The personal voice is presumed to be frivolous, emotional, and nonobjective. The business voice, on the contrary, is always under control, understated, and calm.

Even if we could maintain such clear-cut distinctions in our business and personal approaches, it would not really serve our purpose as communicators. When we interact with others, it is more effective to sound like "flesh and blood" than to try to transform ourselves into robots. Moreover, a certain degree of emotion in our voices and demeanor can help us to be more effective than we might otherwise be. As a public-speaking teacher once said, "When a speaker is *enthusiastic,* the listener will forgive him/her many mistakes; but if the speaker is not enthusiastic, the listener *will forgive nothing!*"

When we discuss some of the messages that cause folks to become angry with us, as we will in Chapter 4, we will see that "neutrality," or indifference, is a culprit. Too often, when we think we are sounding fair and objective, we may be coming across as neutral, uncaring, and insensitive, which makes us less effective.

Building Trust: First Step in Becoming Credible

An obvious handicap in using the telephone is the fact that we usually cannot see the person on the other end of the line. If the caller is not previously known to us, we tend to be a little "suspicious" of him or her because we are not able to watch his/her "body language" to see if he or she is being forthright and sincere with us. According to a number of nonverbal-communication researchers, we tend to judge the honesty of other people largely from interpreting visual cues. Do they look us straight in the eye when speaking? Are there any telltale twitches and involuntary ticks that can be giveaways of their true motives? Do they tend to nervously shift their weight as they talk? These are some of the visual cues we look for to determine honesty, and they are not, of course, available for viewing when we speak on the phone.

Nonetheless, we need to interpret the sincerity of others, as well as appear to be honest to them, when we speak on the phone. How can we build a sense of trust when we have had no prior relationship with the person or when our contacts have been limited?

Self-disclosure

One of the most direct ways of building trust is to "open ourselves up" a little so the other person can "see" who we are. By telling the other person a little about ourselves as soon as possible in the conversation, we can put him/her at ease and facilitate a smoother exchange.

An obvious way of doing this is to announce who we are and the reason for our call in the very beginning of the conversation. If we wish to obtain information from the other party, and we intend to ask questions, it is essential that we *offer some information about ourselves before requesting information from others.* Failing to do so arouses suspicion.

After announcing who we are, it is a useful courtesy to ask the other party how he or she is. The phrasing of this pleasantry is not as important as the tone with which the question is asked. It should sound as if we *are really interested in the answer.* If we sound like so many other canned "Have a nice day" advocates, we will tend to turn off the other person. By asking the person for a response at this early point in the call, we also give ourselves a very good opportunity to hear the person's voice, which will give us information as to how to better communicate with that particular individual. (This will be explored in greater detail when we speak of adjusting our voices to those of others.)

We can build trust by volunteering an innocent observation of our own, such as, "I love days like this, when the sun is shining. They seem to energize me. In any case, the reason I'm calling is . . ." While such an expression may seem to be useless to some, it really helps to build trust because we are revealing a little bit about ourselves to this "stranger." In doing so, we are showing that we are like him/her and that we are "normal." Who *doesn't* like a sunny day, after all? We also provide the other person with an opportunity to say how much he or she likes rainy days, or to say nothing at all. By being open, we are avoiding the appearance of being covert, concealed, and, perhaps, strategic, which make others suspect us rather than trust us.

A word of caution and common sense is needed here. In self-disclosing we are not revealing deep and dark secrets about ourselves but are quickly commenting on something innocent and rather non-controversial. This device is intended to serve as an icebreaker.

Getting Along, Going Along, and Code Switching

There is an old expression used to help new people smoothly enter an existing institution: "If you want to get along, go along." The meaning of this phrase is clear. There are rules and regulations that facilitate interaction, and the wise person recognizes and respects these situational "codes." Such a person also understands that codes are broken at one's own risk.

A similar circumstance exists on the telephone when we speak to another person. The other person is accustomed to interacting based upon certain *communication rules or codes,* which often differ from our own. To be effective with other people, we should (1) recognize what their code is and (2) adjust our listening and voices to that code.

What kinds of codes exist? Perhaps the most common and dramatic sorts of codes are *regional dialects or habits of speech.*

Speaking to Folks in Different Regions

Anyone who uses the telephone while conducting business across the country appreciates the rich diversity of vocal nuances with which people communicate. There are some basic vocal characteristics that seem to change when we speak with friends or associates in the South and the East, for instance. Our friends in the South may prefer a more leisurely approach to speaking, whereas easterners seem to be in a bit of a hurry by southern standards. At the same time, it may be said that very often there is more melody in the southern voice while the eastern voice tends to be less variable in pitch. Some folks report that the volume in these respective voices tends to differ, one being characteristically "soft," the other of greater volume and intensity.

Neither vocal pattern or dialect, it should be pointed out, *is better.* They are, nonetheless, rather different. When we are trying to build our credibility and effectiveness, it serves our purpose to *minimize the perception of our being different or alien to the other person.* One communication scholar claims that our persuasiveness and overall effectiveness with other people are determined by the extent to which we are perceived as being *of the same substance or identified with those people.* If our voices sound foreign to those folks, we will be objects of suspicion and will tend not to be trusted. If our voices and overall patterns of communication "blend" with others, we will create greater identification and trust.

Am I suggesting that we become chameleons and alter our appearance to suit our environment and the needs of the moment? *Yes. It is in our interest as successful telephone communicators to do so.*

For many of us the process of adapting ourselves to others in this fashion is second nature. We seem to do it automatically. A former trainee of mine was so adept at this adjustment process that observers could tell which region of the country he was calling with pinpoint precision, based only upon the manner in which he was communicating at the moment. His approach to Bostonians sounded clearly different from his Chicago presentation. In what ways did his voice change?

There are three basic vocal characteristics: rate, melody, and volume. We can speak faster or slower, in a more expansive or restrictive vocal pitch range, and softer or louder. By selecting one or a number of these characteristics we may better adjust our voices to practically any other voice we hear. This can be done in a subtle way as well.

For example, if I am speaking to one of my friends in the East, I will tend to speed up the rate at which I speak to make that person more comfortable and to create identification. I will not necessarily alter my pitch or volume, though. The alteration of rate, alone, may produce the outcome I wish.

The same principle applies if you are dealing with someone from your own region. Based upon the way the other person says "hello" and the way the person responds to your initial exchange of pleasantries, you should, after practice, be able to *decode that person's preference for being communicated with in a given way.* It is as if each person extends to us a "communication contract," which we can make or break through our accommodation to his or her wishes. We need to increase our perceptual ability to recognize what the person's "offer" or needs happen to be.

If, for instance, a person answers the phone with an abrupt "hello" and seems to snap back a quick "okay" to our inquiry as to how he or she is, the person is telling us to sound concise and be brief. The implication is that our vocal rate should be rather brisk and our pitch somewhat serious. We would be foolish, in such a case, not to respond in this fashion. There is an exception to this principle, though.

If a person answers the phone and sounds dejected or downcast, *it is more effective to contrast our voice with his/hers.* After all, we don't want to get down in the dumps ourselves, do we? We also have an opportunity to bring the person out of his/her prior attitude by sounding a little more optimistic ourselves. It is remarkable to note how people's voices change when we inject a little vigor and verve into our voices. If they start out with a downcast "hello," and we immediately say, with a lift in our voices, "Hello, Mr. Smith?" the person will tend to brighten immediately with a hopeful "Yes!" The secret is to inject our enthusiasm into saying the person's name as a question rather than as a statement. We are also trying to convey the feeling that "it is nice talking with you."

Echo Certain Words and Phrases

There has always been much wisdom in the suggestion that we *try to speak another person's language.* We will never really use language in an identical fashion, but we can help ourselves to be more influential by selecting certain terms in the language of another to echo back to that person.

I See, I Feel, I Hear

It has been observed by students of human interaction that folks tend to habitually use certain words to capture their experiences. For instance, if you ask a person what his opinion of a given politician is, he will probably respond with one of the three following types of statements:

1. "*I* see *John Doe as a person who . . .*"
2. "*I* feel *John Doe* is *a person who . . .*"
3. "*John Doe* sounds *like a person who . . .*"

In other words, most of us tend to describe our experiences in terms of what we (1) see, (2) feel, or (3) hear. We seem to prefer one sensory modality over another when we perceive events and when we describe to others what we perceive. We thus express ourselves through a certain *sensory style.*

The savvy telephone communicator will *detect the preferred sensory language used by another and will adjust his language accordingly.* This will create a sense of identification between the communicators and will build trust.

At the same time, if communicator A uses *visual* language, and an insensitive communicator B insists on telling A how he or she *FEELS* about things, these folks will be speaking at cross-purposes and will be stimulating dissociation rather than identification.

Although the three senses of sight, touch, and hearing seem to be most frequently used by communicators in a habitual fashion, others tend to concentrate on the remaining two senses, taste and smell, to describe their experiences. A former professor of mine in graduate school used to implore her students to "chew on" what she thought was a particularly "juicy" idea. Gangsters in movies are fond of saying that "something smells fishy" about a given situation, and others insist they "smell a rat."

When others use pet terms repeatedly in conversations, we should echo these terms as well and avoid substituting our own preferred word for theirs. Substituting terms may make them feel that you are disagreeing with them or creating distance between them and yourself.

Creating trust, through self-disclosing, code switching, and echoing, is just one of the ways to enhance our credibility and overall influence. In addition to being trusted, we need to sound *expert.*

Sound Like an Expert

If you are like most people, you have probably always admired great athletes, selfless humanitarians, and those most rare of creatures who never seem to be at a loss for something to say, in even the most challenging professional situations. We call these people many things, from "magicians" to "miraculous," yet they are most often regarded as *experts* in their chosen fields. What makes these folks sound so authoritative on the spot? Is it that they are knowledgeable? Not entirely. We can all point to people who undoubtedly possess "product knowledge" or who have at their command armies of facts, yet they do not formulate and share their ideas in a smooth fashion.

Robert Maynard Hutchins, the former head of the University of Chicago, once declared, *"Knowledge is not the possession of facts, alone. It is the* organization *of those facts."* Expertise, in the same vein, is communicated primarily through the appearance of being organized. By developing the faculty of organizing our ideas more efficiently on the spot when needed, we will appear more credible to others and be more effective on the phone and off.

The Magic of the PEP Format

How may we articulate our ideas in a snappy procession rather than have them stumble out of our mouths? One of the most effective organizational techniques I have found is called the "PEP Format." Several examples follow that illustrate this design.

Example A

(Point) The PEP Format consists of three simple steps.
(Evidence)

1. We first make a general statement that we intend to support, which is called our *Point.*
2. Next we invent supporting ideas to make our *Point* sound solid, which is called *Evidence.*
3. Finally, we conclude our PEP Format by restating our *Point* as we first said it.

(Point) As we can see, the PEP Format consists of three simple steps.

Example B

(Point) The PEP Format is the best organizational plan for putting together ideas on the spot.
(Evidence) I say this because . . .

1. It helped me to earn a five-hundred-dollar scholarship in college.
2. It has been applauded by thousands of Telephone Effectiveness Seminar participants; and
3. It is so *easy* to learn and use.

(Point) It should be apparent that the PEP Format is the best plan for putting together ideas on the spot.

Example C

(Point) There are a number of reasons the PEP Format is so effective.
(Evidence)

1. By starting with a point and ending with the same point it reinforces the main idea.
2. It makes the main point sound substantial by supplying evidence to support the point.
3. It is concise.

(Point) Therefore, there are a number of reasons the PEP Format is so effective.

Example D

(Point) The PEP Format should be used in different business situations.
(Evidence)

1. It should be used to formulate statements of policy.
2. It should be used to respond intelligently to on-the-spot questions and challenges.
3. It should be used in letters as well as on the telephone.

(Point) As we can see, the PEP Format should be used in different business situations.

The preceding examples demonstrate at least a few properties of the PEP Format. First, it can be used to *explain or persuade,* depending upon our purpose and our use of the word "should." If we are speaking of what "is," our purpose is usually to explain or inform. When we use the word "should," we are advocating or persuading. Either purpose is easily accomplished through use of the PEP Format. Second, the PEP Format can be employed in a sequential manner, whereby one PEP Format logically follows another. Third, the PEP Format may appear in written form as a tight, logical outline, or it may appear more casually in paragraph form, as it does in this very paragraph. These are some of the properties of the PEP Format.

We will now provide examples of the PEP Format as it is used as a device for responding to questions.

Why does the PEP Format seem to consistently use three supporting ideas in the Evidence Step?

Example E

(Point) The PEP Format uses three supports for each *Point* for at least a few reasons.
(Evidence)

1. Three reasons seem to make an idea sound substantial, as if it rests upon a solid foundation.

2. Three reasons are rather easy to develop.
3. Three reasons are easy to deliver.

(Point) Thus, the PEP Format uses three supports for each *Point* for at least a few reasons.

What happens if you are unable to develop three distinct units *of Evidence to support the main Point? Is it acceptable to use fewer supporting ideas?*

Example F

(Point) It is perfectly all right to use fewer supporting ideas in such a circumstance, as long as you allow yourself some leeway to do so.
(Evidence)

1. In example E we gave ourselves some leeway by saying there are "*at least a few reasons*" the PEP Format uses three supports.
2. The phrase "at least a few" promises that we will come up with two *or more* ideas, so either way, we "win."
3. If we are lucky, and we remember or think of our third supporting idea, we can mention it, or we can bridge from the second idea back to our point.

(Point) Therefore, it is perfectly all right to use fewer than three supporting ideas as long as you allow yourself the leeway to do so.

When using the PEP Format, are we supposed to "call out" the numbers associated with our supporting ideas as we proceed? For instance, should we say, "Number 1, Number 2, Number 3," and so on?

Example G

(Point) Some speakers like to "signpost," or announce their ideas by referring to each number as they proceed.
(Evidence)

1. It enables them to remember their ideas by focusing on where they are at a given time.
2. It makes them sound crisp and especially organized.
3. It helps the listener to remember the points as they are mentioned.

(Point) Indeed, some speakers like to "signpost," or announce their ideas by referring to each number as they proceed.

Do some speakers avoid signposting?

Example H

(Point) Some speakers avoid signposting in certain circumstances.
(Evidence)

1. They wish to have an "off-the-cuff" sound, while really being organized.
2. They may wish to avoid bringing attention to the organizational tool they are employing.
3. They may not be sufficiently confident in the idea they are promoting to bring attention to the fact that they are trying to "prove" a concept or explain a principle.

(Point) Yes, some speakers avoid signposting in certain circumstances.

PEP in the Difficult Situation

Occasionally we find ourselves in situations in which we would benefit from employing an organizational tool on the spot. The PEP Format is very useful for this purpose. Imagine you are answering the phone, and the following dialogue ensues:

Caller: *May I speak with Mary, please?*

You: *May I tell her who is calling, please?*

Caller: *No. It's personal.*

What would you say? Let's assume that you have been asked to screen incoming callers before putting them through. *This* caller is not following the normal "script"! What can you say to clarify and support your request for the caller's name? Many folks in your position have found the PEP Format useful because they may politely insist:

You: *I'm sorry, but I will have to ask who is calling, and we do this for a few reasons:*

1. *It helps Mary to be organized for the call.*
2. *It assures the caller of Mary's complete attention, and*

3. It is a security precaution. Once again, may I please tell her who is calling?

Clearly, this is a more lengthy request for a name than we are used to providing at this point, but in the face of resistance an approach such as this may work when other methods do not. Sometimes callers need to hear "good reasons" for conforming to the most simple requests, and when we are prepared to provide them, their resistance vanishes.

Helping the Disoriented Caller

As mentioned in Chapter 1, we find that on certain incoming calls, those with whom we speak are confused and do not know with whom they wish to speak or the department that can be of service to them. We need to offer some alternatives that can help them come to clarity as to the purpose for the call and the routing it should take. PEP can help here, too.

Imagine you work in an appliance store, and a confused-sounding caller says, "I want to talk about a stereo system." Instead of sending the call to the sales department, which many of us would do right away, the perceptive call handler would check for clarity to determine *which* department and person might be of greatest help. This would save the caller from the frustration of being transferred to a number of extensions where he or she would have to repeat the request for assistance. Here is how the call might proceed more smoothly, using a form of PEP as an information-gathering device:

Caller: *I want to talk about a stereo system.*

You: *Are you interested in:*

1. *Repairing one;*
2. *Purchasing a new one, or*
3. *Getting more information?*

Caller: *Well, it's about the one I bought last week from you people. (Silence)*

You: *May we help you:*

1. *Add to your system,*
2. *Discuss a service question, or*

3. Learn more about how it works?
Caller: *Well, it just quit working.*

You: *It sounds to me like the service department should be able to help you. I'll be happy to connect you with Bill, our service manager,* okay?

Caller: *Okay.*

You: *One moment, please.*

While this sort of exchange tends to remind me of the old game show *What's My Line?* we do find that obtaining information from some folks can be difficult unless we are prepared to offer them what are called "forced-choice questions." Such questions ask for information by providing several categories of response. For example, they might ask, "What is your view of telephone effectiveness training for managers? Do you think it is (a) very necessary, (b) moderately necessary, or (c) not necessary at all?" When we ask such a question, we are *actively shaping the response* while limiting the available sorts of response. Not only is this a timesaving device from the user's standpoint, but it tends to encourage people to provide us with the kind of information we are after.

One participant in a seminar in Cincinnati mentioned that she was having a difficult time getting information from those she was asked to interview by phone. Among other questions, she was supposed to ask business people the amount of their yearly revenues. This is, of course, a rather closely guarded figure and subject for discussion, so she was meeting with a great deal of resistance. I suggested she use a forced-choice question because she was primarily interested in qualifying whether the company was large enough to have a need for certain equipment. If the company earned more than five million dollars in gross revenue, she told me, then the firm was deemed large enough. She reported later that it was much easier to get this information by asking: "Would you say your company is of the size in which it earns revenues above two million dollars or five million dollars?"

The forced-choice question is designed to elicit rather specific information. It is almost opposite to "open-ended questions," which tap into more fluid and lengthy responses. An open-ended question might ask: "How do you feel about telephone effectiveness training for managers?"

The PEP Format, and its variants, can be extremely helpful in projecting the image that we are organized, expert in our area, and credible. People often ask if PEP may be used in repetitious business situations as well as on the spot. Absolutely. In fact, I suggest that folks use PEP as a short-order formula for organizing complaint calls, product inquiry calls, and explanations for others who call us. It enables us to distill the essence of a thought while delivering it in its most potent form.

Having discussed how we might be perceived by the other party as trustworthy and expert, we are now ready to explore how we might cultivate vocal dynamism, the third element of telephonic credibility.

Wanted: Dynamic Telecommunicators!

Earlier in this chapter we mentioned that folks tend to have a split personality at different times. Face to face, they are dynamic and full of life. When they pick up the phone, however, they lose the verve and excitement that they project interpersonally. This presents a real problem and challenge for all telecommunicators.

The telephone is a more difficult and demanding communication medium than the face-to-face communication channel. When we speak in another person's presence, we are assisted by thousands of nonverbal communication cues that help us to process and transmit messages. Nonverbal nuances such as hand gestures, for example, help communicators to *accent* what they are saying; *regulate* the command of the communication channel by indicating that the speaker wants to talk or is not yet finished talking; *bolster* and *emphasize* what is being conveyed; and *replace language* when necessary to arouse a special sense or meaning. Facial expressions provide speakers with *valuable feedback* from the listener, which indicates whether the listener is *really responding* to what is being said; the *attitude* of the listener toward what is being conveyed; and the *general interest level* of the receiver for different aspects of the subjects communicated. Clothing itself arouses all sorts of meanings.

Without these cues we are "flying blind," as seminar participants describe their challenge as telecommunicators. The absence of a visual dimension to telecommunicating invests us with the difficult task of *training our voices to do the work of the missing nonverbal nuances.* Our voices, in the telephonic situation, bear a *burden of expressiveness.* We need to be more dynamic on the telephone than we are in person, in a vocal sense. It is perhaps ironic that we should reverse our apparently split personalities and put our better selves forward through this medium.

Developing Your Power Voice

What are some of the vocal behaviors within our control that we may alter or enhance for the purpose of telecommunicating in a more dynamic fashion? There are six basic vocal attributes: speed, volume, melody, pausing, clarity, and attitude. Through greater proficiency with these nuances, we can seem as more credible and powerful.

Speed

As noted earlier, the average American speaks at a rate of 100 to 150 words per minute. The average listener, on the other hand, has the capability of *listening at a rate of 600 to 650 words per minute.* A moment of reflection will probably give you a clear idea of the communication problems that commonly occur because of these different listening and speaking speeds. If listeners have such a great capacity for processing speech, and most speakers do not satisfy that capacity by speaking at a fast enough clip, listeners are going to become disinterested and tune out. This happens all the time when we are on the phone. Listeners are really appreciative of those who seem to know what they are talking about and get to the point. In other words, listeners reward speakers who speak at a faster rate, within reason.

Some seminar participants have reported that telephone companies suggest that *when they communicate by phone, they speak even more slowly than they normally do.* I believe this tip will increase telephone company revenues while making the communication gap wider. *We should strive to increase the rate at which we speak by one fourth to one third* and at the same time achieve a high level of clarity through the proper articulation of our language. In other words, we should take care to avoid garbling our words in the interest of speeding up the rate at which we speak.

Volume

I am fond of the television commercial that says: "If you want to get someone's attention, just *whisper.*" It's true. Whispers are magnetic. They draw us closer to the speaker with a compelling force. They also have a rightful place in telecommunication.

As part of the split personality referred to in other sections, we tend to "flatten out" our voices when we get on the phone. A part of this process of making the voice less rich and dimensional is speaking at the same volume throughout a call or during a number of calls. In short, what we tend to do is *drone* in a monotonous fashion.

We should try to use different levels of volume during our calls for the purpose of keeping the listener awake, as well as to add dynamism to the content of our message. It is great fun to develop the sixth sense, which can tell us that another person is on the verge of "tuning us out" during one of our monologues. What we can then do is increase or decrease our volume in a substantial way, and our partner will suddenly seem to come to life again!

Melody

Speech teachers and music teachers are fond of telling their students that most of us use very little of our "native expressive ability." Assuming we are blessed with functional vocal equipment from birth, we can develop a rich, expressive quality if we know what contributes to this outcome.

A major component of voice is the range within which we can emit various "pitches." To illustrate this range, we might hear at the highly expressive end the disc jockey, whose voice is fluid, constantly changing, and reaching magically from the lowest note to the highest within very few words. At the other extreme, we hear the classical "monotone voice," which is very restricted in range and which most folks call "dull." Currently, most of us fall in the less interesting range. Fortunately, though, we can practice using our voices in more interesting ways and improve. Vocal dynamism is learned, in other words.

A first step toward greater expressiveness is to try to "feel" what it is we are saying as we are saying it. We should concentrate on dramatizing what we say. This does not mean we should don costumes and use other "props," but we should try to gradually add more life to our voices and language. Allow your voice to convey your personality. You may find that relations with others become easier and more interesting.

Using a tape recorder can be of tremendous help as well. You might practice reading paragraphs from the newspaper. At first, read a story into the tape recorder as you would normally present it to another person. Without turning the tape recorder off, repeat the story with more vigor and melody added to your voice. Play both renderings back. You will probably note immediate improvement, which can be accelerated through continual practice.

Pausing

In Chapter 1 we mentioned that it is a good idea to *pause in the middle of a sentence rather than at the end*. We said that this technique would help to manage time and better control the conversation.

Pausing in the middle of sentences also helps us to sound more dynamic on the phone. This practice lends to our ideas a sense of momentum, which is interrupted when we pause at the ends of sentences.

It should be noted, of course, that *excessive pausing will create a boomerang effect*. It will make the voice sound choppy, which will frustrate and agitate the listener.

We should also avoid pausing immediately after we have made a negative or sensitive statement, especially if we are looking to discourage resistance from the listener. If we are in the position of mentioning something negative, to take the sting out of the statement, we should try to follow it up with a neutral or mildly positive statement before pausing. This will reduce resistance and discourage untimely interruptions.

Clarity

It is especially important that we strive to be extremely clear when pronouncing and delivering words on the telephone. Because the listener cannot read our body language or literally watch our lips, we are required to exert more effort in articulating, or satisfactorily uttering our language.

One of our tendencies as telecommunicators is to assume that the microphone in the telephone receiver will amplify our voices in such a way as to make unclear speech more clear to the listener. As computer programmers are fond of saying, "Garbage in produces garbage out." The equipment will not do the work of our lips, teeth, and gums, which are known as our "articulators."

We also "clip" our words at their beginning or ending. For example, we might seem to be saying "'ompany" when we mean to say "company." We also compress our words and leave out syllables. We will say "*compny*" for "company." A particularly frustrating practice for the listener is when the speaker trails off at the ends of words or sentences. "Tomorrow," the speaker might say, "we are going to have compan. . . ." As listeners, we may never decode what the speaker was really trying to communicate.

An excellent model for articulation is presented by former Congressperson Barbara Jordan, of Texas. She sounds dynamic, in part, because her language is articulated so clearly. As we have often heard about some speakers, "She could read the phone book out loud and sound impressive!" What is her technique? Among other nuances, Ms. Jordan seems to put an "ah" sound at the ends of her lines-*ah* and words-*ah*. This assures that they can be understood clearly by her listeners-*ah*. Actors and other public performers are taught this technique to help them be understood in the back of large meeting rooms when there is little or no electronic amplification of their voices. It is a habit worth emulating on the phone. We should add this embellishment in a subtle way, in order to help us retain a smooth overall delivery.

Building a Positive Attitude: The Telephone Smile

Unless you read any number of self-help books that discuss the merits of enthusiasm and positive thinking, you would not normally connect these qualities with successful communication. I believe strongly that we will help ourselves to be much more successful with others on the phone and off if we convey positiveness in our tone of voice while projecting the desire to make the person on the other end of the line feel that he or she is a valued person. Some folks call this attitude "caring"; others call it the *telephone smile.*

We can all recall telephone conversations with folks who have been able to quickly "unmake our day." They convey that chilling blend of indifference and negativity. What a "downer"!

Fortunately, there are others whom we encounter with good feelings because they project warmth and interest immediately upon answering the phone. They use the telephone smile. These people consciously *remember to put a smile on their faces before picking up the phone.* Instantly, a "lift" is given to their voices, which makes the call proceed in a smooth fashion. Some companies are so concerned about conveying smiles over the phone that they have placed mirrors before those who answer the phones so the "operators" may see their own expressions as they speak. One of my clients in the hotel business has inscribed these words above the mirrors: "Would *you* rent a room from this face?"

Some folks insist that giving away a smile to a stranger is beyond their responsibility in answering the phone. I do not think this claim has merit. Others insist that forcing themselves to smile is artificial and not natural. I am fond of the line "I will take a phony smile any day over a genuine frown!"

By constantly looking to improve our dynamism through development of the voice, as well as by enlisting trust and organizing our ideas, we can appear more credible and be much more effective in our telecommunications. We are now ready to see how we can enhance customer relations through conflict management.

4

Customer Relations: Handling Telephone Conflict

The Scene: Your Office
The Time: Friday Afternoon
The Situation: A call comes into the office on line 3. Your officemate yells out that it is Mr. Frisbee on the line, and he sounds mad. You think for a minute. What could he want on a Friday? "Oh, no," you mutter under your breath, "his shipment probably didn't arrive on time. He's going to kill me!"

Your stomach starts knotting, and you suddenly feel weak. Maybe you should tell your office buddy to get rid of Frisbee. Tell him anything! You're away for the weekend on a desert island with no phones! Nice thought. Forget it.

You feel like turning the call over to someone else, but he is one of your accounts, and you will just make him angrier, which he is becoming right now because you have been keeping him on hold for the last two minutes while worrying. "There's no way out of this," you think. "I think we're going to lose his business this time. We've been late with his shipments one time too many. Hey, this isn't my problem! It's his. What am I getting so crazy for? Feeling emboldened and dizzily indifferent, you decide to make believe there is nothing wrong at all. "He can flip out—that's his business. I just work here anyway." Clearing your throat, you practice saying hello with just the right amount of composure. Your hand reaches for the phone, and just as it arrives, the light on the button stops flashing! Frantically, you grab the phone and blurt out a hello—to a dial tone.

Your worst fear is coming true. You have to call him back and deal not only with his anger with the late shipment but with his apparent disgust with your having kept him waiting. Right now you would trade your job for a chance to fight Sugar Ray Leonard! Your odds would be better. As you dial Mr. Frisbee's phone number, you wish a genie would emerge from a bottle and grant you just three nifty conflict-management devices that you could use on him. No way.

You already know that Frisbee is about to ruin what was going to be a wonderful "escape holiday" over the weekend. As always, you are going to stew about your "chat" with him, and curse him and your job a thousand times, feeling ever more powerless each time.

Suddenly your thoughts are interrupted. Frisbee answers the phone himself! He does sound mad, you think. . . .

Is this scene familiar to you? If you work in a customer relations capacity, as many do who are involved in manufacturing, retailing, and the service industries, this kind of event may seem too common.

I once heard a businessman discuss his approach to client relations. He said, "No business is without dissatisfied customers. They are unavoidable." At the time I heard this remark, I thought it was a little bit of a cop-out. Perhaps *this* businessman was accepting a higher frequency of complaints than he should have been experiencing. A second thought on the subject convinced me otherwise. If we do a sufficient amount of business to be profitable, we will probably rub someone the wrong way or not come through with a promise or commitment as we should have. It does, indeed, seem inevitable. Further, communication researchers and psychologists are telling us these days that conflict is normal. *The absence of conflict, in one form or another, is unusual.* This marks a rather dramatic change in our basic assumptions about human relations, doesn't it?

Conflict Is Okay?

"Conflict," in the most concise way, may be defined as a "disagreement." This failure to see things eye to eye may be the result of different views, evaluations, values, goals, interests, message strategies, or "personalities." Any number of processes may get in the way of smooth relations with our clients and associates.

One of our many problems in dealing with conflict, according to experts, is our basic assumption that it is "unnatural" and "abnormal." Nothing could be further from the truth. Conflict is always with us, in one form or another, simply because it is impossible to see the world, in any of its facets, precisely as another human being does. Our view of events and our attitudes are going to differ slightly from those of others. A "perfect match" is simply not possible to obtain, or at least to maintain for very long. We need to realize that "perfect understanding" is truly exceptional. We must lower our expectations of the communication process while increasing our efforts in strategic ways to produce greater success in dealing with clients and others.

Conflict, while being temporarily uncomfortable, can be very productive. It is a form of feedback, which tells us that something is going wrong somewhere. If we did not receive this sort of response from our clients, we would be repeating past mistakes without any idea of the results. Corrective action would be difficult to implement. Moreover, conflict can stimulate different ways of approaching problems and challenges that we would not have discovered otherwise. While we strive for smooth interpersonal and business relations, we should expect and plan for the inevitable turbulence that is to come. By treating such events as normal and predictable, we will be in a much more constructive position to deal with them effectively.

"What We Have Here Is a Failure to Communicate!"

What are those things that seem to be causing so many of our misunderstandings? Some of our troubles are the result of our communication practices. Here are some of the main culprits.

Misinterpretations

Having written and received many contracts in business, I can tell you that misinterpretations of the contents of these agreements is commonplace. One party might write a word that is crystal clear to him, but causes nothing but headaches when another party tries to interpret the meaning of the term.

Communication scholars are quick to point out that meanings are "in people, and not in words." Words are only conventional vessels that we send to others, hoping that our counterparts will "fill" those vessels with the proper meanings and assign them correct or desired interpretations. Words fail us too often, though. If I say the word "dog," what kind do you see? A German shepherd? A poodle? If you "saw" one of these breeds, you would have been wrong! That's right; *wrong!* I had in mind my little Doberman pinscher, who is one of the best canine joggers and ballplayers in Glendale, California.

Would it really be appropriate for me to call your association for the word "dog" *wrong?* No. Your meaning for the term is completely appropriate because it is yours. If I, as a speaker, do not take into account the very high probability that you will hear the word "dog" and see something other than a Doberman, I would be making *an incorrect assumption.* Assumptions contribute significantly to misunderstandings.

It should be noted that the word "dog" is clear in one sense. We all recognize that the concept of a dog is that of a creature that is usually friendly to humans, uses four legs for locomotion, and emits a barking sound. This is clear. What happens when we use less graphic words, like "service," "loyalty," and "quality"? The likelihood of misinterpretations multiplies tremendously.

Miscues: Using the Wrong Terms

Most of us have had the experience of thinking about one thing and saying its opposite. This happens frequently when we offer directions to another person. We say, "Turn right at the stop sign and continue for about ten miles." The person follows our directions and becomes lost. We look at the transcript of our directions and say, "You should have turned *left.*"

One of the best remedies, especially in the case of receiving directions or instructions, is to repeat very slowly your understanding of the directions. This permits the other person to catch mistakes before they cause problems and inconvenience.

We also create misunderstanding by using *vague or ambiguous terms.* If we find ourselves using terms such as "perhaps," "maybe," "possibly," and the like, we are probably going to confuse the listener. It is a good idea to check with our listener for clarity, to make sure that we have reduced uncertainty to the extent that it is possible in the situation. I like the phrase "Just so I've been clear, do you have any questions at this point as to how we are going to proceed?" This places the burden of clarity on my shoulders, and not upon my client's. I avoid conveying the feeling that I am saying, "Do you understand me, you dummy?" This is accomplished by emphasizing the idea that "I've been clear."

Accents, Dialects, and Regional Differences

Some of us have difficulty understanding speakers from different regions of the United States and the world. We may try to take extra care to listen to them, but it sometimes does not help us "decode" what is being said. Many seminar participants have expressed frustration with this "clashing of two worlds." Some folks tend to *blame the "outlander" for his/her manner of speaking.* This sort of attitude leads to increased misunderstandings and conflict.

If you find yourself in the position of taking calls from folks from a particular country, or who speak a different language, there are a few things that can be done.

The company may elect to hire and train someone who speaks the language. You might wish to bone up on some phrases that help you to expedite business, though your intention is not to become fluent in the language. You might also ask the speaker if there is someone else at his/her location who can speak English, or your language. Using alternative and additional communication channels, such as memos and letters, to clarify the intentions of the caller may be helpful.

We should avoid assuming we understood the person, without repeating to that person what we think we heard. This technique, as you know from Chapter 2, is called "active listening." It can prevent many misunderstandings.

Fighting Words

Many of us deal with clients who use vocabularies different from our own. Sometimes these folks use terms that we consider profane. Such terms might be the proverbial four-letter words, or they might be other *fighting words* than rankle us. "How *dare* you say that to me," we think when we hear the offending term.

We tend to stop listening to the speaker after hearing such

language. We "fight back" in silence as he or she continues speaking. Finally, when we do speak, we fail to point out that certain terms make us uncomfortable and settle for injecting a certain tone of hostility into our voices. Through this process we *cause* conflict, where there may have been none, or we *increase* the existing level of conflict. We do not have to respond nonconstructively or hostilely when we hear such fighting words. As we will see when we discuss methods of coping with irate callers and conflict, we can control how we respond to this sort of provocation.

Problem Personalities

Often we encounter people whose personalities are what we consider abrasive. Such folks might come on too strong when we answer the phone or have a demanding tone of voice, by our standards. Whatever is happening, one thing is for sure. We are responding negatively, and we almost feel "doomed" to do so. It may seem as if the situation has gotten out of hand before we recognized there was an ill feeling between ourselves and the other person. How could this sort of thing happen so quickly?

I have a hunch that many of us make a "shopping list" of personality traits we seriously dislike in others. Our shopping list begins with the words, emblazoned in stone, *"I hate people who. . . ."* We then follow these words with any number of practices. For instance, we might claim, "I hate people who start out by saying the words 'You people.' " Or, "I hate people who don't tell me who they are right at the beginning of conversations." These statements, by the way, have been uttered by numbers of folks in seminars.

The problem with such strong statements is that they *predispose us negatively toward people who use certain statements or words. We create a "negative-response contract" with ourselves.* We say the equivalent of, "If anyone says, X, Y, or Z, I will respond in an inappropriate way." We seldom disappoint ourselves. People persist in saying such things, and we persist in responding inappropriately.

This habit of "blaming" our customers for their behavior will be discussed in greater detail when we speak about how we can control our own attitudes. At this point, though, we can say that this habit is worth breaking.

Breaking Bad Habits and Starting New Response Patterns

Typically, when we are in a conflict situation, we respond in an unproductive fashion. We either resort to a "quick-fix" solution, or we make the conflict worse by delivering poor service to the client while processing the complaint.

Five Negative Responses

When in a conflict situation, or in anticipation of one, we tend to resort to one of five negative responses: avoidance, withdrawal, denial, compromise, and retaliation.

As in the example at the beginning of this chapter, many of us think of *escaping* from the difficult situation and use this device to deal with conflict. Our first impulse upon hearing that we have an angry customer on the line is to blurt out to our officemate, "*You* take the call! Tell him I'm not in, or I'm in a meeting, or something!" By avoiding the painful call, we tell ourselves, it just may go away. This is obviously not a constructive approach to handling a conflict call.

Withdrawal, the close relation of avoidance, is not a favorable approach either. Withdrawal frequently occurs when the employee claims that "it's not *my* job to handle this kind of flak. I'm going to transfer this account to my supervisor. He's *paid* to handle this type of situation!"

Denial is assured to make the conflict worse. The client has regaled us with a full description of the complaint and indicates that he or she is very angry with us. We respond with a phrase such as, "You don't really mean that, do you?" Implied in our question is the suggestion that the client has no right to feel angry with us. *Warning: If you really wish to increase other people's anger, tell them they have no right to be angry. They will angrily prove you wrong.*

We are taught to admire the "peacemakers" in our culture. The road to peace between competing factions and persons, we learn, is *compromise.* You give a little, as the expression says, and you get a little. This is the nice, easy, and democratic way of handling misunderstandings, right? Not really. We can all point to conflict situations in which our choices of action were severely limited for any number of reasons. We might not have been able to strike a compromise, if this was our wish. To put it a little differently, we cannot "give away the store" or any part of it sometimes. In certain encounters a compromise could actually keep both parties from reaching a better understanding or outcome. The biblical story of Solomon the King comes to mind. Two women come to him claiming to be the mother of a child. He determines that compromise is the best remedy and declares, "Cut the child in half!" Clearly, this is not a satisfactory outcome, though it does have the appearance of being equitable. (I am told the idea here was that the true mother would not have allowed such a thing to have occurred and would have cried out, "Give it to the other woman." Nonetheless, in certain circumstances, compromise is not the most highly valued conflict management device.)

Our most unconstructive approach to the conflict call is to *retaliate,* or fight back. Upon answering the phone, we hear a voice yelling at us. What is our "natural" response? Yell back. It is second nature, it seems, to echo the emotions being expressed by the angry caller. The problem with this kind of reaction is that it will escalate the misunderstanding to the point where a solution may be impossible.

In addition to these poor responses to conflict management, we tend to employ other behaviors that make the conflict call worse and get out of hand.

Practices Guaranteed to Make Things Worse

1. "Let 'em cool their heels!"

When I ask seminar participants how they currently handle the caller who is "hot under the collar," the response I most commonly hear is, "I let them talk themselves out, and when they are good and ready to listen, I talk." This technique may have some merit in certain situations, where the caller is emitting a "blue streak," but it is inappropriate in many others.

If we "fall silent" when a caller is telling a woeful tale, he or she may think we are: (1) indifferent, (2) not really listening, or (3) playing a game with him/her. If any of these interpretations is made based upon our conduct, we are probably going to fuel the resentment of the other party.

Rather than being virtually mute, we should offer periodic feedback in the form of such phrases as: "I understand that," "Yes," and "Uh-huh." These minimal cues will tell the other person that we are supportive of their explanation, though we may not be in complete agreement with the position.

2. "I'll just put 'em on hold. That will make 'em more civil and respectful!"

If the hold button is, as one seminar participant called it, "the greatest money-maker the phone company has ever devised," it is also one of the most irksome, especially to the already alienated communicator. People are impatient when put on hold. When they are kept there, they grow angry. When they have a complaint to make, and they perceive that they are being obstructed in making it known, they become livid and unmanageable.

The hold button should be used sparingly, and if you intend to leave someone waiting in the limbo of hold for very long, you may wish to schedule a call-back with the person, instead.

3. "I'm going to transfer you to accounting." (Who knows, you may get lucky and find someone there who can really help you.)

Incessant transfers from one extension to another in an organization can try the patience of a Zen master. When we believe we have a situation for which there is no clear person in mind to best handle it, we should promise a call-back and do some research on our own before suggesting a different routing for the call. If we have an angry or hostile person on the line to begin with, and we proceed to play the electronic equivalent of "hot potato" with him/her, we will escalate the conflict quickly.

4. "I simply cannot afford to take my time with this call. I have two other lines waiting!"

There are few behaviors that strike us so rudely as when we are being rushed off a telephone call. This is especially the case if we have called an organization for the purpose of lodging a complaint. We want some *sympathy* and *stroking*. As the complainer, we believe we are the most important person in the world at that moment, and *we have been wronged!* If the party to whom we are emoting rushes us, this tells us we are not important, and our "calamity" is not serious. We then determine that "we'll teach them to take me lightly! Who is your supervisor?"

We need to make a judgment in a situation where we seem to have an angry customer on the line. The issue is: Do I offend this person further by attending to my other calls by rushing this one, or do I take my time with this one, while risking the wrath of the incoming callers who are waiting on hold? This is a good, old-fashioned "bind," wherein we seem to lose no matter what we decide. Nonetheless, I suggest we either: (1) take our time with the irate call or (2) promise and deliver a timely call-back when we may devote more attention to him/her. The risk of severely alienating a customer should be avoided, even if we believe we will temporarily inconvenience a few others.

5. "Look—they only pay me to answer the phones here. They don't pay me to be nice and sweet to everybody."

As you may have gathered, this phrase represents a rather sour attitude. I have actually heard customer relations people say things such as this, and mean them. Unfortunately, negative attitudes are easily conveyed over the telephone. If we deal with angry customers by expressing unhelpful, disinterested attitudes, we will make difficult situations worse. We should try to express a certain degree of pleasantness at all times, while understanding that such tones are part of our jobs.

6. "Don't ask me where your freight is! I only know what my computer terminal tells me. How could we lose the shipment? Oh, I don't know. Actually, I think they do it with mirrors. . . ."

It is the rare person who can delicately introduce "gallows humor" into a difficult situation and have a customer appreciate it rather than resent it. Our statement above is almost a direct quotation of a customer relations person whose characteristic approach to communicating is through *sarcasm.* As a communication device, sarcasm introduces difficulty into the interpretative process used by the listener. What sarcasm in our tone of voice says to the listener is: "Don't take the meaning of my words literally. Take my tone of voice as your interpretive guide." As you can imagine, when a customer does not know whether to take the messages of a businessperson seriously, it causes confusion and frustration. It makes obtaining needed information unduly complicated.

> 7. *"I am not going to put up with this caller any longer. I'll trick 'em. I'm going to start to speak and hang up on* myself! *He'll never figure out that I hung up on him!"*

This "cute" little trick is guaranteed to "flip out" the client who either: (1) knows this childish prank or (2) reads this book. You would be surprised how many folks use this device to avoid conflict situations. While claiming that the client is more calm after the trick is used, I tend to believe that the risks are not worth any apparent gain.

We should take care in transferring calls and in handling the phone at all times to minimize the possibility of innocently disconnecting a party as well. Any delay in handling a complaint can result in negative feelings.

> 8. *"I didn't hear you. Would you repeat that?"*

This translates to the listener: "I wasn't listening to you, because, frankly, your situation is not important enough for me to give my undivided attention." Clients and callers do not appreciate it when we seem to give our attention to distractions within our office while ignoring the person on the line.

> 9. *"I know I promised to call back today, but I simply don't have the information I thought I would have at this point. I'll wait until I have something to say."*

If I could create a rule for all time, it would be: "To the extent possible, *always* call someone back when you have promised to do so." Few things irk me as much as folks who break their call-back promises. The reason is that we tend to set our schedules and calendars based upon the promises of others. If I am promised a four o'clock call, I will discourage other activities within that time frame. If the call does not come on time, or fails to come, I have sacrificed valuable time. If I am trying to obtain information for a client by a certain time, and I have not been able to complete the task, I will call the person to let him/her know my progress and set another target for delivery of the information.

10. *"Mr. Jones, the problem was not with* this *department. If you really want to know who blew it, it was the shipping department, as usual."*

We should avoid laying blame upon others within our company for a problem we are attempting to solve. It may be accurate that the shipping department does many *bozaic* things, but it is really not the type of information that should be communicated to outsiders, for it diminishes the credibility of the entire organization.

11. *"Well, Mr. Sandwich, what happened was we booked your order, sent it to your address, and it was refused. Now, Mr. Sandwich, before we can send it out again . . . What? Your name isn't Sandwich; it's Saskewitz? Oh. Maybe that's why the order didn't make it. . . ."*

People take their names very seriously. This is especially the case when they are lodging a complaint or are in a difficult customer-company situation. There are few of us who are totally insensitive and undisturbed when we hear our names mispronounced. If we are uncertain about someone's name upon hearing it over the phone, we should make a little excuse and request the spelling and pronunciation of it. For instance, we might say, "I'm sorry, we have a little noise here. Would you please spell your name for me? I didn't quite catch it. Thank you." If we can get the person's name correctly at the beginning of the call, we can refer to him or her by name during the remainder of the conversation, which suggests a "personal" approach to the matter.

12. *"This static on the line* is *terrible. What were you saying?"*

If we have a poor telephone connection, we should offer to call the other person back and report the problem to the telephone company, which will probably arrange credit for the poor connection. If we use an "unclear" communication channel, we do so at our peril. Noise on the line is frustrating for both parties, and may inadvertently lead to increased ill will. If your problems with noise continue over many calls, call the phone company and insist upon a test of the line. Tell them you are losing money by the minute. Unfortunately, it will probably be a true statement.

> *13. "Operator. May I help you? Yes, I guess Ms. Jones is away from her desk. I'll try another line. No, I'm sorry, I can't take messages. They will have to take one in their department. Why, then, does the call get transferred back to my board after five rings? That's because of the new telephone equipment we just purchased."*

I suppose it is a part of the American genius to develop technologies to solve human communication problems. The telephone, of course, helped us to transmit information across great distances without taking horse and buggy along. Currently, there is an explosion of growth in telecommunications technology. Several types of telephonic switching devices are available to companies that wish to cut costs and streamline operations. Sometimes, however, companies make massive investments in equipment *that is more disturbing to its users than it is helpful.* "Automatic call-forwarding," which is a feature of many systems, can be very confusing to the caller. Let's say I program my phone to transfer all calls to the shipping department, where I intend to be for a few minutes. After completing my business there, I go to another department. My calls are being answered, "Shipping Department," which confuses the caller. Moreover, if that department is unaware that I have programmed my phone in this way, they may assume the caller made an error, or the switchboard person did. It also puts the shipping people in the position of having to be "operators," which they are not. In other words, this device may confuse matters more than be of assistance.

Some systems contain a "beeping feature" that lets the employee know when he or she has been on the line "too long" with a given call, or when another call is waiting. Many folks have expressed the feeling that they are being "controlled" and that the time limits artificially imply that there is a "perfect" amount of time with which to handle each and every call.

Others report that their systems have so many gadgets that they don't have any use for most of them. In other words, the company may have "overbought." Unfortunately, because of the large investment represented in purchasing many phone systems, a company is probably stuck with its purchase for a long time.

We should take greater care to think through the impact of a new phone system upon our clients and the public. Though we may seem to be saving money by making a conversion, we may at the same time set ourselves up to lose more money by choosing a device that causes ill will and inefficiency.

Having discussed some of the problems that cause conflict, as well as are "guaranteed" to make it worse, we are now ready to examine some constructive approaches to managing the difficult call and the conflict situation, as well as our own attitudes.

Handling the Conflict Call: Several Options

Even though many of us have no control over the initial *causes* of the conflict situation, we are called upon to *troubleshoot solutions.* There are several devices available for managing the difficult person on the line, as well as for keeping our own "heads on straight."

Create a Supportive Communication Climate

One of the major obstacles we confront in conflict situations is *defensiveness. Defensiveness* may be defined as *responding to practically all the messages we hear during a given call as if they are* personal attacks *upon ourselves.*

What happens is rather simple. We are having a conversation with another person, and we hear a message that we think is aimed at us; at our personality. What do we do? If we are like most folks, we immediately try to figure out: (1) why we are under attack and (2) how we may effectively attack back. As a result, we are no longer trying to achieve a solution for a problem, but *we* become a problem, as does the other person, who started the verbal barrage. What ensues is an increasing cycle of attack and response, resulting in extreme alienation, unless the cycle is terminated. The pattern of negativity may be ended by starting a *supportive message process.*

"Let Me Introduce Myself: I'm Count Dracula"

The defensiveness cycle reminds me of Count Dracula. First, he bites us, and then we are doomed to bite back or bite someone else. We can recognize this creature's approach by identifying the types of messages that we find threatening.

According to researcher Jack Gibb, there are six types of messages that cause folks to become defensive: evaluation, control, strategy, neutrality, superiority, and certainty.[1] As we discuss these messages, you might try to remember the last time someone used these messages on you, or the last time you might have inadvertently communicated one to another person.

Evaluation Most of us are sensitive to being criticized. This is especially the case if the criticism we are hearing is aimed at us on a personal level and is not addressing the matter at hand. Imagine being a customer relations person answering the phone and hearing the following words:

Caller: *You people are really something! I placed an order with you three weeks ago and you lost it. Now you are telling me I am going to have to wait for another week! Boy, I think you must try awful hard to mess things up!*

Note the *personal* nature of the criticism being levied here. The words "you people" and "you" are repeated. It would be easy to take this sort of language personally. The caller seems to be focusing more on the personalities involved in the matter than upon the solution to the immediate problem.

The clear temptation we would have to resist, upon hearing this sort of language, is to criticize or evaluate back. This would escalate the conflict.

Control We also resent language and messages that suggest to us that we are being "controlled" or dominated by another person or organization. When we tell people what "you'll *have* to do" and seem to offer no alternatives in a situation, we tend to make folks suspicious and put them on their guard.

Sometimes statements of "policy" are defense-producing because they sound so controlling. "Our policy is that you will have to bring in your receipt, fill out a refund form, and discuss the matter with the manager before we can authorize a refund. Then you will have to wait ten days to receive your check by mail, because we cannot issue one without our home-office approval."

Most of us wish to be accorded a degree of dignity and be made to feel that we are self-directed people who have choices in a situation. "Control," as a message strategy, denies us this feeling of independence and freedom of action.

Strategy When we perceive that others are being strategic with us, we become defensive. They may be keeping essential information from us by answering questions in an evasive way. Sometimes folks feel they are being manipulated or toyed with in this fashion when they "go through screening" after requesting to speak with a certain party. The common response, "And may I ask who is calling?" is often thought to be a concealment device, whereby the caller may be "rated" and either connected with the requested party or "screened out." As we will see in the next chapter, we should avoid "turning off" the caller through this sort of strategic phraseology.

Neutrality If we project the feeling that we are completely neutral toward a situation, we will cause the other party to feel threatened and alienated. Our neutrality may easily be interpreted as indifference or apathy, which will be regarded negatively.

Sometimes, as communicators, we sound "neutral" to another person when we are trying to sound businesslike and objective. In fact, many of us have been told to eliminate traces of emotionalism from our voices when we speak with others for business purposes. This instruction may be helpful in certain circumstances, but as a general rule, it is counterproductive. Some emotions, such as enthusiasm and even alarm, may be helpful in communicating the importance of a subject to another person. By "neutralizing" our voices we risk being misunderstood and deny ourselves expressive capabilities.

Superiority We live in an "egalitarian" society in many ways. When the country was founded, in fact, there was an effort made to eliminate aristocratic titles and offices. This tradition of equality is perceived by many of us to be a birthright that we do not give much thought to—until someone violates this legacy by becoming *superior* with us in tone of voice or in message content. We then respond almost automatically with resentment and with efforts aimed at "showing him/her that he or she isn't so high and mighty."

Superiority is often communicated when speakers find the need to "credential themselves" by listing their superior credentials for us. "In my twenty years in this business, and after having taken twelve college degrees in this precise area, I can confidently state that I have never suggested such a course of action as that which you are presenting. It also violates my refined instincts as a multimillionaire, philanthropist, and ballroom dancer!"

I was a part of the single largest United States Navy training project some time ago, and I decided to illustrate this idea about superiority by saying: *"Just take it from a Ph.D in communication, former college professor, and nationally recognized expert!"*

I asked a burly captain who was sitting to my left what he was thinking as I credentialed myself in this way. He slowly lifted his head and said: "I was thinking, *stick it in your ear!"*

Clearly, superiority causes dramatically negative responses.

Certainty A special sort of resentment is shown toward the person who claims "to know it all." This is the one who claims to possess the one and only answer to a particular human problem and will not consider alternative approaches.

Such a person is comfortable issuing ultimatums to others: "Now, this is the way it is going to be because I know what the right approach is here!"

If a person insists that there is only one answer to a human problem or situation, he or she is probably wrong. When we are exposed to such dogmatic personalities, we tend to get "sucked into" the problem by summoning all of our energy to prove him/her wrong. In other words, we become certain *that he or she has the wrong answer, and we will not rest until we have proven this to be the case!*

Supportive Alternatives

Instead of evaluating the other person or trying to exert control over him/her, we should attempt to use descriptive language and define the problem, apart from personalities. Rather than initiating a complaint on a personal level, such as we did in a previous example, we would attempt to eliminate criticism aimed at the other person. For example, we might say, "It appears that getting my order on time is continuing to be a problem," rather than starting the call in an accusing way with, "You people are really something!" We are not playing the childlike game of tag, in which our goal is to make the "it". Focusing our energies upon the person instead of the problem to be solved creates a defensive cycle or perpetuates an existing one.

You may be asking yourself at this point, "What if somebody calls me a bozo, or some other four-letter word is used in reference to me? I don't have to take that, do I?" I cannot set a policy for all companies, but it is helpful to be as supportive as possible in all situations. Let's imagine a person calls you and says: "You people are idiots! You can't seem to get the simplest order right. I specifically asked for my order by Friday, so I could get it to my client. It didn't come, and I looked like a buffoon! All because of you. . . ."

I would suggest the following sort of brief response: "I am sorry you were inconvenienced, Mr. Jones. Now, let's see where we can go from here. . . ."

Note several features of this concise response:

1. We do not respond to the party's name-calling.
2. We make a brief apology, which tells the party that we are not indifferent to the situation.
3. We focus upon the solution to the problem by *projecting the matter into a future course of action.* We say, "Let's see where we can go from here."

The key to this type of response is that we are *deflecting the attack rather than reflecting it.* We are consciously choosing to react in a positive manner, although the person is provoking us. This kind of response requires practice to develop and become comfortable in using. It is worth it, though, because it frees us from the need to "bite back" when the other person strikes at us.

If the other person insists upon discussing the indignity to which he or she has been exposed, we can listen to the lament and respond with: "Fine, now let's see where to go from here. I suggest . . ." After a while the problem focus that you are taking will hold sway over the personality orientation of the other party, and you should be on the way to solving the problem.

Instead of trying to sound cool and neutral, we should attempt to sound supportive through the use of *empathic messages.* These statements tell the other person that we care for his/her feelings as well as for our point of view. Introducing such phrases as "I'm sorry" can be a great help in making the other person feel we care. I recognize that *you* may not have been the original cause of the problem, but offering a brief apology can make the other person feel better. The normal human tendency, when we hear someone say he or she is sorry, is to offer forgiveness. A comedian decided to walk down the street in New York City and randomly approach strangers and say, "I'm sorry." Approximately nine out of ten times he was "forgiven" by the strangers, who said, "That's okay, don't worry about it."

Other empathic messages that can be used are transition phrases such as:

Well, I understand that . . .
Well, I recognize that . . .
Well, I appreciate that . . .
Well, I know what you mean . . .
Well, I respect that . . .
Well, I agree with that . . .

These statements create a supportive climate by showing our concern to the other party while responding in a personable manner.

Instead of sounding *strategic,* we should strive to project *a tone of spontaneity.* We should appear to "have all of our cards on the table," rather than be thought of as concealing information from the other party. Introducing a bit of lightness into our voices can help us to avoid the somber tones of the cloak-and-dagger artist.

Superiority may be profitably replaced with *a sense of equality.* If we are a party to a problem, and especially one that requires remedial action from the other person, we are wise to involve him/her in the solution to the problem. Often, people call us and lodge vehement complaints and are prepared to offer constructive suggestions as to how we might settle the problem, but are never given the opportunity to share their idea. We might simply ask, "What can we do to set things straight?" This question might temporarily throw the other party, but upon recovery, the party may be very generous in offering an extremely equitable solution from our point of view.

Instead of seeming to be completely *certain* about a given circumstance, we should try to appear more *flexible* if possible. This is the case even if we truly think there is only one course of action available to us. In seeming to be flexible, we arouse a sense of "ownership" of the solution by the other person because we do not seem to be forcing it upon him/her. We might put it in this manner: "Francis, I think we are going to find that the best approach is to sell the stock right away, unless you can think of a better alternative. I might remind you that time is of the essence at this point."

This approach tells the other party: (1) we have a pretty good idea for action; (2) it can be overridden by a better idea; but (3) the new idea needs to be aired right away, to be adopted. The other party feels a sense of involvement in this method, where he or she does not when the speaker is responding with "certainty."

Avoid Four Types of Messages

Our discussion of defensive and supportive message strategies has revealed, through examples, four types of messages that we should explicitly avoid using to solve conflict: name-calling, ultimatums, either/or propositions, and shaming statements.

We should resist calling people names, as well as categorizing their firms through use of disparaging labels. Sometimes we are "name-calling," though the explicit term is not mentioned. This happened to me when I was trying to follow up on a late order from one of my suppliers.

> Gary: *I ordered some materials a while back, and they haven't arrived. Can you look into what may have happened to the order.*
>
> Them: *When did you place the order?*
>
> Gary: *Several weeks ago. I would say it was about April fifth."*
>
> Them: *And when was it promised?*

Gary: *By last Friday.*

Them: *Well, you should have gotten your order in a few weeks earlier if you really needed it by Friday.*

Gary: [*getting exasperated*] *But they promised.*

Them: *Well, if it had been in a few weeks earlier, you would have had it by now!*

You might be wondering where the name-calling was in this conversation. Well, I got the impression that I was being called "tardy" or "late" with my order, though this word was not mentioned. As you no doubt gathered, it was absurd for the person with whom I was speaking *to blame me for expecting them to process an order on time!* When we discuss the "burnout" process that public-contact personnel go through, we will return to this issue of "blaming our clients," which was taking place during this call.

Ultimatums and either/or propositions are closely related, and should be avoided. As mentioned, the ultimatum is the closest we can come to verbally using force with another person. We are declaring, "This is the way it will be!" The either/or says, "This will be it *or* else!" The latter provides the illusion of choice in the matter, when there really is none. Both types of messages are strongly resented by listeners.

The "shaming" message is designed to raise the specter of possible embarrassment before our peers or superiors. One such message might be, "Wait until they hear what you just said at our association meeting!" Another way of potentially shaming someone might be by saying incredulously, "You don't want to *go on record* as having said that, do you?" When we think someone is going to quote us out of context, or repeat our statements for the purpose of vilifying us, we get angry at the suggestion.

Active Listening Reduces Emotionalism

As noted in the chapter on listening, one of the best devices for achieving clarity when dealing with others on the phone is by using the technique known as *active listening. Active listening is repeating to the satisfaction of the other party what you think he or she meant.* Also known as "nonjudgmental" listening, this process helps us to de-escalate the emotionalism that can become intense during a conflict call. Our intention here is to repeat what we think the person *means, not the exact words that are being spoken.* At the same time we avoid adding to our interpretation of his/her words any negative or positive judgment of our own. By doing so, we avoid increasing the conflict by making the person less likely to fully disclose his/her point of view.

Imagine receiving the following complaint call:

Caller: *I want to talk with somebody about this blasted account of mine.*

You: *It sounds like you're pretty upset about it. Am I right?*

Caller: *You bet I am.*

You: [probing] *Is this something that just happened?*

Caller: *No, it's been going on for too long now.*

You: *I'd like to know more about it, if I may. You say it started a while back?*

You may have noted the effort made here to draw out the person, who was not positively predisposed toward telling the facts of the story. Through a process of repetition and probing we stand a good chance of hearing the facts and diminishing any nonproductive emotionalism.

Metacommunicate!

Sometimes our conflict calls are so severe that we wish we could bring in a referee to impose some rules in the arena of combat between ourselves and the other party. This is not really practical, but we can play dual roles ourselves, functioning as ourselves and a referee, by *metacommunicating. Metacommunicating is a way of opening a new channel of communication between ourselves and another, when the existing channel is blocked.* It is a way of surmounting an obstacle between ourselves and another party, by bringing attention to the obstacle while offering a method of overcoming it.

Imagine another person is swearing at you on the phone. Although you know "you are not paid to take this kind of abuse," you also recognize that you are really expected to be able to handle yourself in this kind of situation. As you listen to the profanity, you grow increasingly upset. You quickly reach a point at which you are concentrating more upon the prospect of hearing added abusive terms, and this expectation takes your attention away from helping the speaker. The swearing is causing a blockade in the communication channel. It is up to you to open an additional channel with the person by metacommunicating. You could do this by saying:

"Mr. Jones, I want to help you, but I am having a tough time listening right now because of the number of four-letter words that are being used. If we could reduce that number, I'd be much more comfortable as well as able to help you, which is what I want to do. Okay?"

A legal secretary reported to me that she was having a conflict with her boss, though it wasn't out in the open. He asked her to "screen all of my calls when they come in, but don't screen my friends when they call." If you think about this set of directions for a moment, you will probably conclude that he gave her an impossible mission. How could she *know who was a friend or foe without asking?* Her boss, in other words, put her in a "bind," from which she could see no possible escape. She asked me what to do. I suggested she metacommunicate by saying:

> *"Boss, I want to do a good job and follow all of your directions. It seems that I am prevented from doing so by directions that seem to cancel each other. I have been asked to screen all calls when they come in, but not screen your friends. If I screen* all *calls I will inevitably screen some friends too. If I screen no calls, I will not offend any friends, but I will be letting nonfriends through, as well. I will be pleased to do one or the other, which is possible, but it appears that no person can do both. I do want you to know that I want to do a good job and will appreciate your help with this procedure."*

There is a risk involved in metacommunicating. We are pointing out that all is not "rosy" on one level. Sometimes folks do not want to hear that there are any problems. This situation requires that we metacommunicate about the "rule" the other party endorses, which says, "Don't bring me any news of problems." We might have to begin our statement by saying: "I recognize that you may not be comfortable hearing about a subject such as this; however, it is important enough to warrant your attention."

Metacommunicating is an exciting technique because it helps us get "above" our ordinary method of communicating with another person, in an effort to improve how we communicate with that person. In this respect, it is a device that can quickly change relationships by altering the "communication contracts" formerly enacted between the parties.

I was having a conversation with a person representing a large organization. I called for the purpose of following up a letter I had written. Before I knew it, I found I was being wrongly accused by that person of all sorts of peculiar deeds. I really wasn't prepared for this barrage. I said to myself, "You're the 'expert.' What technique will you retrieve from your bag of tricks to reduce the conflict here?" I decided metacommunicating might work. It did.

I said to the other person, "We're having an argument right now, aren't we?" After receiving acknowledgment of this, I continued, "Let's put this aside for a minute, if you don't mind. I have some questions I'd like to ask you about another subject." I proceeded to ask questions about areas of interest to this person's institution, which were happily answered. After a few minutes I suggested we "return to our argument." My associate said, "I wouldn't call it an argument. I'd rather call it a *discussion*." I agreed to this change of interpretation, and we proceeded to clear up our misunderstanding and negotiate a better agreement than we would have had without the "discussion."

In this encounter I said, in essence, "We don't have to fight like this. In fact, let's talk about something else for a while. The fight will 'keep.' " We were able to open a new communication channel which was much more relaxed and conducive to exchanging ideas.

Avoiding "Burn-out"

One of the built-in occupational hazards of dealing with angry and upset people day after day is that we can grow distant to their problems. This process of becoming less eager to help the client has been called, among other things, becoming "burnt-out." This "condition" or attitude can become rather pronounced when customer relations people find themselves *blaming the client for his/her misfortune and making it difficult for the client to obtain satisfaction.*

Public contact professionals who interact with hostile calls find that they need to: (1) identify with the caller sufficiently to solve his/her problem; (2) act as the company's or organization's agent and look out for its vital interests; while (3) not becoming too "close" or "distant" to the company or customer, where the interest of one is placed above another. This is quite a lot to "juggle" at once, and many folks err in one direction or the other. They become too close to the customer and compromise the position of the firm, or they side with the firm and behave as if the customer is always "wrong," until proven correct.

If you find yourself blaming clients for their "stupidity," or if you approach calls, over time, with greater negativity and alarm, you might be experiencing the process of alienation known as "burnout." One of the remedies that can revitalize our commitment when this occurs is *role playing.* This is a technique whereby we *actively imagine what it is like to be a caller or client with a problem. We try to identify the feelings he or she experiences and capture a sense of what it is like to be in "his/her shoes."* This simple imaginative exercise can help us to become resensitized to the needs of others when we find we are growing callous.

I experienced this "burnout syndrome," as it is sometimes called, after teaching college for a number of years. Like many new professors, I was initially charmed by the image and mission of the profession. I found, however, after a few years, that I was growing more estranged from my students, while my identification with the "professional field," or the world of my colleagues, was increasing. I was becoming, in other words, a straight "company man," and my "customers" were not getting the quality of attention they had received in years past. I found myself *expecting each entering class of college students to be getting smarter, whereas statistics were claiming a contrary trend was taking place!*

At some point in this process, I recognized that I was not having the sort of good time that I once had. I decided to do a bit of role playing to see if I was missing something in my attitudes and approach. I asked myself, "What is it like to be an entering college student, anyway?" I rather quickly remembered my first year in school, which was a little "squirrelly." I was scared, and all kinds of new social skills were required. At the same time, I had to deal with professors who would not chase you to complete assignments. In other words, I did not have a perfect first year. How could I ask others to have one?

I believe I caught myself through this process of role playing in time to make some valuable adjustments in my approach. This does not mean that the standards of achievement were lowered. It did mean that I implemented friendlier and more supportive methods to help people work within those constraints.

When All Else Fails, Admit Blame!

I will never forget having a conflict call with someone who really ended up teaching me a lesson. I had agreed to present a seminar through an institution that promised to send out 200,000 announcements of this event in the mail. This was, at that point in my experience, a dazzling commitment! I had visions of overflow crowds screaming to get into the program while constables restrained the swelling masses. In any event, the date of the program was approaching, and I had not heard any news from the institution that we were breaking attendance records. In fact, I had heard absolutely zero from them. I decided to get them on the phone!

Upon calling, I discovered my contact person was off somewhere doing a little fishing. This did not reassure me. I requested he call me, which he promptly did. It was apparent from his voice that he didn't like being "hooked" back to work. I asked him if there were any problems in promoting the program. After looking through the catalog, he said my course had been omitted. Left out! I asked how this kind of thing could happen. After a long pause, he said, "Well, I guess we just blew it. I'm sorry."

For a moment I wondered what name I was going to call his organization and behavior. Summoning all the restraint I could, I asked, "Well, what can we do at this point?" He started to mention all kinds of promotional possibilities, some of which we later implemented, which caused the program to be successful, after all. To this day, I have to give my associate credit for being big enough to admit blame in a straightforward fashion. Had he hemmed and hawed, or if he had tried to cover up the errors, I would have grown angry to the point where I would not have asked about salvaging the program. In other words, he helped me to return to a constructive orientation, which promoted our mutual success in the situation.

It should be noted that admitting blame should be done in circumstances where it will not put you or your company into a court of law!

Handling Sexist Remarks

A number of women in my seminars tell me that they often hear sexist remarks from some of their clients and other callers. A few examples of these remarks are:

"And how are you today, little girl?"
"I don't want to speak with a woman!"
"Let me speak with a man!"
"Look, honey, maybe I'd be better off speaking with your superior."

This list is in no manner exhaustive. The question I hear is, "How can I deal with these remarks?" There are a few possibilities.

1. *Bring immediate attention to the offensive language and insist that the person desist in its use.*

This is one of the most direct, yet volatile responses one can make. You will certainly be clear that you are being offended, and some people will apologize and alter their approach. At the same time, you risk "blowing the client out of the water" and losing his business. (I am assuming that the great majority of sexist remarks are made by men, ergo, the word "his." This does not mean that women are immune from this problem.)

2. *Agree with the speaker and continue as if nothing offensive was said. In other words,* deflect *the comment.*

The transition phrases introduced in Chapter 1 and repeated in this chapter may help. Imagine the following exchange:

Caller: *Look, honey, I'd be better off speaking with your superior. Would you put him on?*

You: *Well, I appreciate that, but this matter is within my province. Now, let's see where we were . . .*

Caller: *I don't think you get my meaning, little lady. I want to speak to a man!*

You: *Well, I respect that, but I am assigned to your account, and what we will do from here is this . . .*

As you may have noticed, transition phrases may be used to bridge a number of exchanges. In this case, we "agreed" with the speaker, temporarily, before asserting our method of handling the matter. We did not "take him head on," nor did we argue the merits of his sexist remarks.

Some women are comfortable enough with these kinds of calls to introduce a little humor into the proceedings.

Caller: *Look, honey, I'd like to speak with the boss. Would you put him on?*

Woman: *You're speaking to* him. *Let's see how I can help you.*

There is special resistance, it seems, to dealing with women within some of the historically "macho" trades, such as the building industry, and in manufacturing. One seminar participant mentioned that she has a tough time convincing men that she is the *plant manager* and oversees a great number of activities. She finds that she elevates her credibility and earns respect by engaging in a brief technical talk with the man, which alerts him that she "really knows what she is doing." Many men, in such situations, are asking for other men because they assume they will be "wasting their time with a female." The woman who can use "buzz words" and jargon from the technical area of the industry can assert her qualifications in short order.

I believe in the school of thought that suggests we try to rise above provocations of this sort to the extent that it is possible. From my point of view, we are not in business to "teach people lessons" or to expand their consciousness about serious social issues. Friends, family, and spiritual leaders may attend better to these matters, perhaps.

I have a good friend who wants me to invest in his restaurant. I have a lot of confidence in him, but his approach to the business concerns me. When I asked him what sort of restaurant he wished to open, he said, "French or Spanish; it doesn't really matter." This seemed all right to me. He then started to tell me how he was interested not in serving good food that people liked, but in uplifting people by *teaching them about exotic dishes and raising their consciousness about what they were eating.* His idea was to *really talk with people about their food.*

When I eat in a restaurant, my number-one concern is good food, and my second is to be left alone. I do not wish to be interviewed or "tested" later about the cuisine and my sensitivity of palate. I feared my friend was falling victim to what psychologists call *the secondary gain trap. He was saying he wanted to be a successful restaurateur, but he was really hoping to be a successful food teacher.* In other words, he seemed to be putting a relatively secondary gain ahead of the primary one—making a successful enterprise. We can also fall into this trap if we insist on teaching people lessons instead of expediting business as our primary objective.

Controlling the Conversation Inconspicuously

Some of the techniques discussed in the first chapter on managing time by telephone may be used to handle conflict calls as well. As noted in the last section, *transition phrases may be used as bridges from what one person says to your response. They may also be used to gently obtain control of the conversation.*

As you probably know, some folks take a great deal of time to make their complaints. Often we cannot afford to listen to their "complete and unedited version" of a story. In short, we need to interrupt them to discuss certain relevant items. A good way of "seizing control" of the conversation in a diplomatic way is to use a transition phrase as a way of interrupting the person after he or she has concluded a phrase or thought. Here is an example:

Caller: *And then I thought it was going to come on the next day, and then the next, and it never arrived . . .*

You: [*interrupting*] *Well, I appreciate that, yet let's see exactly what happened to your order. Do you have your account number handy?*

Breathing in the middle of a sentence will also help you to avoid being interrupted when you need to deliver some facts or data to the listener. These two techniques are facilitative in nature and should not be used to excess within the same call.

Keeping Cool: How to Handle Your Own Attitudes Toward Conflict

Sometimes conflict calls seem to get out of control, and we find ourselves getting personally involved and very upset. This may happen to some more than others, yet many folks reach a boiling point "from which there is no return." In other words, *we become the problem.* How does this happen? What can we do to avoid getting out of control ourselves?

According to a number of psychologists, at the root of our emotional reactions is the endorsement of one or a number of *false beliefs or statements we tell ourselves* about how the world *should* work and how other people *should* behave toward us. For instance, we might believe, as many do, that "nobody should use profanity or four-letter words when speaking with me." We insist they *shouldn't do it,* though they seem to do it rather frequently. We also tell ourselves that it is *"awful when people swear at me, and it makes me very upset."*

By telling ourselves these things, we set ourselves up for a strong emotional reaction, which causes us to become upset. All that needs to occur is for a person to swear at us, and *we will make ourselves very upset.* We tell ourselves, "*He* upsets me" or "*She* makes me mad," when in reality we are *choosing to become angry at what we consider to be "awful" behavior.* According to some psychologists, we could "reprogram" ourselves to become *calm* or to respond much less negatively when we hear that sort of language. It is also pointed out that there are few things in life that are so completely intolerable as to deserve the designation "awful." We choose this sort of highly emotional label, which does not really apply to the gravity of the situation. We would be better off labeling the language "uncomfortable" or "displeasing," rather than "awful." Our reaction would probably be less extreme as a result.

This applies to many situations, including those that arise outside of conflict calls. When we insist strongly that something shouldn't be a certain way, and we grow angry as a result, we are choosing that emotion and are responsible for how we feel. Other people are not causing us to feel a certain way.

One of the major proponents of this view is Dr. Albert Ellis, who is very much worth reading. Among his many books is *Humanistic Psychotherapy: The Rational-Emotive Approach,* which probes some of the ways that we cause ourselves to become upset by endorsing false beliefs.[2]

Some negative statements people endorse are:

1. *We need to be* perfect *in every human activity to consider ourselves worthwhile.*
2. *We need to get the love and approval of* everyone *in order to feel good about ourselves.*
3. *We need to blame and punish people we consider to be "evil."*
4. *Other people cause us to be the way we are, to act as we do, and to feel the way we do.*
5. *We can't change. If we have been doing things in a certain way, we are doomed to repeat the same pattern of behaviors.*
6. *Other people cause us to be happy or unhappy. We have little choice in the matter.*

As this list implies, we are not going to be successful with each and every conflict call we handle. This would be an unreasonable expectation. We will also encounter people who seem to "break the rules" and get away with it, in respect to their management of such calls. The intent of this chapter has been to *increase our choices within the conflict situation.* With more choices we are more likely to select the most effective one.

I am reminded of the late, great baseball player Roberto Clemente, of the Pittsburgh Pirates. Clemente could do a number of things effectively. He was a marvelous fielder, who had a "rifle arm." He was also an excellent, though unusual hitter. What made him such a threat to the opposition was his ability to hit not only good pitches but also bad ones. It seemed that wherever the pitcher threw the ball, Clemente could hit it. He could even hit wild pitches out of the park for home runs.

When dealing with conflict over the phone, we cannot predict what other people are going to "throw at us," but we can choose the most effective response. And sometimes we, too, can hit bad balls out of the park for home runs.

Notes

1. Jack R. Gibb, "Defensive Communication," in *Nothing Never Happens,* K. G. Johnson et al., (Beverly Hills: Glencoe Press, 1974), pp. 275–78.

2. Albert Ellis, *Humanistic Psychotherapy: The Rational-Emotive Approach* (New York: The Julian Press, 1973), p. 37.

5

The Telephone in the Professional Office

Whenever we see a photograph of a business office, what implement do we see first and most often? The typewriter? No. The stapler? No. Pens? Pencils? No, again. The most commonly photographed item is the telephone. Executives make sure to have photographs of themselves that are destined for release include one shot of the "boss on the horn." The telephone is so indispensable to the smooth operation of a contemporary business that we take it for granted. And this is where our troubles begin, as well as our most pressing business communications challenges.

I suspect that more business deals are "soured" by poor telephone communications than by any other factors. Unfortunately, it is impossible to state precisely the dollars that are lost each year to this practice. We all can point out offices, though, that grate on us whenever we ring them. Perhaps it is the indifferent or "canned" voice on the other end that discourages us, or it could be the outright rudeness of some places of business that turn us off and cause us to redirect our business to more helpful firms. Why is the state of office telecommunications so dismal at this point?

I believe we take the telephone for granted for a few reasons. First, it takes no special training to use. Anyone can pick up a phone and place a call. Second, we have regarded the telephone as a poor substitute for a face-to-face encounter and have decided the scope of business that may be conducted through use of the medium is limited. Third, we believe that communication is easy and noncomplex, so it is undeserving of further attention. Fourth, we believe "telephone work" *per se* is of inferior status, and thus we are reluctant to spend money and effort in training folks to be more effective with this tool.

Imagine the following situation. You place a call to a well-known glass manufacturing company and a pleasant voice answers the phone. You ask for a given party and tell the receptionist your name is Tracy Smith. The voice thanks you and puts your call through. Three years later, you call the company again, after having not spoken with anyone there in the interim. The voice answers the phone, "Acme Glass, may I help you?" You ask for a given party without announcing your name. The voice instantly replies, "How have you been, Mr. Smith?" You are floored by the fact that this person remembered your name after having heard it only one time, three years ago! Does this sound impossible? It does. This is a true story, though. The company had the great fortune to have employed a person with an outstanding acoustical memory. This receptionist was also vitally interested in treating all callers as individuals as a part of the "service" the company offered to clients. Unfortunately, the great majority of telephone communicators do not share this person's enthusiasm. Those who do are exceptional people and are exceptionally valuable to their organizations.

One of my accounts is a well-known medical center in California. The person who receives incoming calls there is remarkable. She tries to make the entire hospital function more effectively by thinking through the impact of her telephone manners upon the whole working system. For example, if she gets someone on the line who speaks in an especially soft tone of voice, she will say: "I'm sorry, we have a little background noise going on here. Would you please speak a little louder for me?" Invariably, the other folks comply happily. She could have easily said: "Speak up! I can't hear you." Or she might have criticized them with the common statement, "Your voice is too soft! Will you speak louder?" She avoids these phrases because she senses that they can be taken as insults, and she goes out of her way to make the caller comfortable. When a caller asks for a doctor who is having a lunch break, she doesn't tell the caller that the doctor is at lunch, but rather than he or she is with a patient and is expected to be free for a call at such and such a time. Why does she do this? She says she thinks it is better if the doctors seem to be busy working all the time. The medical center supports her unique style because it gets so many compliments on her telephone manners.

Office Productivity

Because of poor telephone communications, offices are not nearly as efficient as they could be. In an era in which we have been told that worker productivity is steadily declining, we would be wise to explore those procedures that may be implemented to turn the tide. What can folks do to become more effective telecommunicators in the office while presenting a better public image to clients and prospects?

Basic Telecommunications Policies

Many corporations and public agencies are vigilant in their function as "gatekeepers" of information. Organizations not only determine which messages enter an organization via telephone and other methods but also screen letters and other representations made by their staff to the "outside world." It is common practice in some organizations to have attorneys and communications supervisors review business correspondence before it leaves the premises. The reasoning is rather straightforward. These firms do not want to suffer the inconvenience and potential losses that might result from inaccurate or poorly conceived messages being "officially transmitted" as company policy. Consequently, form letters and outlines are created and disseminated within the organization to serve as guidelines for communications. A certain uniformity of output is deemed desirable, and any concomitant "loss of individuality" is considered insignificant. Deviations from the accepted format are questioned and need to be justified.

This seems like a rational process. Why is it, then, that firms are reluctant to establish and enforce *basic telecommunications policies?* I suspect the notion is harbored that telephone communication involves *some aspect of free speech, and by asserting a communication policy, a company may be violating the rights of employees to this constitutionally protected privilege.* This thinking is counterproductive.

When you call a particular office and reach a certain person, you might hear that person answer the phone with the word "Hello." This is too casual for a business greeting. If someone else had answered the phone, you might have heard, "Hello, Acme Company, how may I help you?" Obviously, the second greeting is much more helpful and is more likely to make the caller feel that he or she is important. By allowing both types of greetings the company is running a risk that a poor image will be conveyed with each ring of the phone. The same ring could signal an opportunity for the firm to show off its professionalism.

I believe all firms, private and public, should make a commitment to upgrading telecommunications practices. The first step is to identify those behaviors that will facilitate business and promote better public relations.

21 Telephone Tips for the Office

The following list of tips for better office telecommunications is offered with the idea that having a coherent policy for answering phones, taking messages, and handling calls, in general, is to be preferred over "winging it." This list is not written in stone, however. Some of the tips that appear here may not suit your organization, and others may. I suggest you *use this list to stimulate discussion within your organization, as well as to arrive at your own set of techniques.* By opening a discussion you will be able to explore current misunderstandings and inefficiencies as well as generate commitment for new practices.

1. *Put on a "happy voice."* Before you answer the phone, you should consciously try to put a smile on your face. I know this may sound artificial at first. It is known that "attitudes" are very accurately conveyed over the telephone, though we may think the other person has no way of knowing how we feel. They cannot see our faces, but, according to nonverbal communication research, our voices give us away. If we allow ourselves to be "down in the mouth," our counterpart on the phone will pick this up and be discouraged from doing business with our firm. At the same time, if we adopt the "telephone smile" and offer it to callers, our communications will proceed more smoothly.

   Some companies believe in the power of the "telephone smile" so much that they have placed mirrors in front of employees so they can self-monitor their expressions, and have placed "SMILE" signs in work areas. Before I get on the phone in the early morning hours, I force myself to smile. It does help my calls.

2. *Try to answer all calls within four rings.* One of the most annoying things to callers is to be left waiting for a phone to be answered after it has been ringing several times. Callers wonder if they dialed correctly. They might also think that the company is on a permanent lunch or work break.

Receptionists sometimes claim that they have to handle such a volume of calls on so many incoming lines that it is impossible to answer all calls within four rings. Should they cut short the service they are giving to calls already answered to attend to new calls? No, they should not. The company should consider investing in a "backup" receptionist if the volume of calls is excessive. Otherwise, the overworked telephonist will be put in the position of committing more errors, which result in greater customer dissatisfaction.

3. *When answering the phone, greet the caller pleasantly and identify your department and/or name.* "Communication department, Dr. Goodman speaking. How may I help you?" This would be a satisfactory way of handling the call because it eliminates a guessing game about the extension that has been reached and the person with whom the caller is speaking. I also prefer the phrase "*How* may I help you?" instead of "May I help you?" The word "how" seems to be more specific, and the user seems to be more prepared to help at that moment. It is also a little distinctive, which is desirable in its own right.

4. *Try to personalize the call in a dignified way.* One of our most cherished possessions on this planet is our name. When uttered in kindness by another person, our name is capable of summoning warm feelings in us while making us instantly comfortable. It is a good idea to use another person's name during the course of a call. It gives the party the feeling that he or she is an individual, and not a number.

One might also refer briefly to a fact about the person. For instance, if you were told by the caller that he or she was planning a vacation, when the person calls the next time, you might inquire, "How was your vacation?" By making a brief, tasteful reference, you will show that you really listened to the person in the past and thought enough of him/her to remember this personal fact.

5. *Apologize for any delays or errors.* This is especially important if you have had to keep the person waiting on hold for a long period. "I'm sorry for keeping you waiting" is a nice way of returning to the line. You may also try, "Thank you for your patience." Both lines acknowledge that there may have been some discomfort suffered through a part of the call.

If the person tells you he or she has been transferred a number of times without speaking to the appropriate party, you might apologize and assure him/her that you will not transfer the call again. To keep this promise, you might have to do a little intelligence work of your own after promising to have someone return the party's call.

6. *If you must leave the line to gather information, give the other party the option of holding or being called back.* The hold button is an overused feature on the telephone. Often we put people on hold almost automatically, even when we intend to be away from the line for periods up to ten and fifteen minutes. The hold feature should be used as a *temporary expedient, not as a "place itself."* We will show respect for other people's calendars by giving them the choice of holding or receiving a return call within a short period of time. They are then free to pursue other affairs, and we can be complete in our mission for information because we are not worried about offending the person we have sent into "electronic purgatory." Further, the other party will be more tolerant of us because we have predicted for them how long the delay will last. We might announce the option by saying, "Fine, Ms. Jones, it will probably take me about four minutes to look that up for you. Would you like to hold, or would you prefer I call you back with that information?"

7. *Always try to fulfill a promise to return someone's call or call someone back.* Of all the negative telephone practices I have encountered, the failure to return a call as promised ranks at the

top of the list for me. I suppose the reason is that I actually *wait for the call, and feel like an utter bozo when it fails to come!* As a result, I have declined several alternative activities during that time slot which might have been productive.

I recognize the fact that some folks promise to call us with certain information by a given time, but when the clock strikes the appointed hour, they are still information-free. Instead of telling us, they decide to call us when they have the information, because a call before then would be a waste of time. This thinking is incorrect. If we have promised a call at a certain time, we should make the call, if only to alert the other party to the fact that we will need more time to gather the promised information. This is a courtesy that people appreciate.

8. Avoid using abrupt questions and phrases. A sampler of impolite and abrupt phrases follows. I might say in advance that this list is suggestive, and not in any way exhaustive.

- *"You can't do that!"* This little gem denies someone the right to proceed in a given fashion. It also sounds harsh and demanding. By emphasizing the fact that "*you* can't" do such and such, the speaker places undue emphasis upon the *doer* and not enough emphasis upon the act. For instance, a less volatile statement might be, "I'm sorry, but that sort of thing isn't acceptable." Though still making a prohibition, we take some of the sting out of the statement in this manner.
- *"You'll have to . . ."* This compulsory statement is one of the closest ways that we can come to doing verbal violence with another. The words "have to" are so forceful that they sound like an ultimatum, which folks resent.
- *"What do you want?"* This crass question could be effectively moderated with the words "May I ask what you want?" By introducing this gentle prelude we sound more courteous and are very likely to get an answer to our inquiry.
- *"Speak up! I can't hear you."* While it is rather frustrating to speak with those who speak too softly to be heard clearly, it only makes the situation worse when we demand the person

elevate his/her volume. If the person is shy, the statement will cause him/her to be more reticent, which is not what we want. "May I ask you to speak a little louder, please? I am having a little difficulty hearing you. Thank you." This request is taken more graciously.

- *"What?"* I recognize this little question does not seem like a tremendous offender at first glance. Said with a certain amount of incredulity, however, this word can ridicule the other party and sound awfully harsh. If we really missed something that was said, we would be better advised to say, "I'm sorry, would you please repeat that for me? I missed it. Thanks."
- *"Who's this?"* This is another demand for information. It may be all right for children to use with each other, but this kind of language is too casual. "May I ask who this is?" is a preferred phrase.
- *"Hang on," "Hold on,"* and *"Hang on a minute, will ya?"* These are little dictators. English teachers would tell us that implied commands precede these phrases. "*You will* hang on," is what is being said here. The forcefulness of the phrase is apparent. I prefer the question "May I ask you to hold, please?" I have found people respond better to this kind of request.
- *"He or she is still out to lunch."* This phrase reveals more than a caller needs to know about someone else's habits. By saying someone is *still* out to lunch, we make it appear that the person is giving him/herself *an extremely long lunch.* Sounds like possible hanky-panky here.
- *"He or she is out to coffee."* Coffee breaks are innocent enough, aren't they? Not really. Imagine that a caller asked for you during your morning coffee break and couldn't reach you. The next time the person called, he or she was told you were "out to coffee" again. After a while the caller might think you are in the coffee business! I prefer the catch-all phrase "I'm sorry, he seems to be away from his desk for a few minutes."

A general principle is to *soften* commands and edicts in such a fashion as to make them sound less harsh. Your efforts will be rewarded.

9. *When taking a message, note several things:*

- *Correctly spelled name.* "Smith" may be spelled four ways of which I am aware. Other names, of course, are much more likely to be mispelled, which can cause problems.
- *Area code, phone number, time zone (if long distance).* If you find you are promising to ask an associate to return a call to a party who is in a different region, ask the party what the local time is. This will help your colleague to return the call in plenty of time. I have had others promise I would return someone's call "by end of day," when their end of day came at 4 P.M. my time! I was placed in the position of breaking the promise, which was embarrassing.
- *Time of the call.*
- *Short reason for the call.*
- *Date.*
- *Your name.*
- *Whether a return call is requested.*
- *Tone of voice of the caller.* This provision does not appear on most message pads, though it is potentially important. I always ask people who take messages for me to be sensitive to the voices of other parties. Their voices can tell me what sort of negotiating position I am in at a given time, as well as reveal their attitudes to me via another person. This provision also serves as a reminder to telecommunicators that sensitive listening is an important part of their jobs.

10. *When leaving your desk or office, tell an associate where you are going and when you expect to return.* This also applies to trips down to the water cooler. Such brief excursions can turn into mini-vacations and major powwows if you run into certain people on the way. By informing a cohort about your itinerary you will enable him/her to sound confident about your physical location and will facilitate the routing or returning of calls. Without such information, officemates are put in a position of sounding uninformed and less credible. This reflects negatively upon the entire staff, including yourself.

11. *When a call comes in for an associate who is on another line, place the call on hold and put a brief note before your associate with the caller's name.* Avoid needless shouting, which can interrupt the smooth flow of the other conversation.
12. *Always try to say "thank you" after processing an order for goods or services, and try to say "good-bye" or "bye" before leaving the line.* When we have been dealing with clients over a long period, we tend to forget these common courtesies. They make a big difference in the client's perception of our eagerness for the business and desire to be of service.
13. *Do not hang up too quickly, in the event the other party has a last-second remark to make.* I call this the "Columbo" effect, from the old television show. Often folks have "just one more thing to ask" about a given situation, and are frustrated when the dial tone tells them it is too late to broach the subject. By allowing a second after the conversation has concluded, before we hang up, we will provide our partner a chance to ask a last-second question or make a final remark.
14. *When leaving a written message with another party, ask for feedback to verify that the message was recorded as you wish.* When others take messages for us, they often distort what we are saying or forget to record essential parts of the message. We don't have a chance of catching their errors unless we ask for some indication of the accuracy of the message they transcribed. Some of us are too bashful to ask for this important feedback, but we should get over this in the interest of clarity. I like the request "Just so I was clear, would you please read back to me the message? I appreciate it." The other party is more than willing to do so in most circumstances. We should avoid asking, "*Can you* repeat that message for me?" Such phrasing places undue emphasis upon the other person's capabilities.

It is sound practice to use this technique when leaving procedural or transportation directions with a third party. The likelihood of botching directions seems to be astronomical!
15. *When disconnected during a call, you call back if you placed the original call, and wait to be called back if the other party placed the original call.* This is what etiquette suggests we do. An obvious difficulty comes if one party is familiar with this rule, and

the other party is not. Imagine waiting for a call for an hour based upon what etiquette says should happen. If you find the other party has not called as required by this little rule, do everyone a favor by calling him/her again.

16. *Try to be polite with everyone, including those who are not especially polite with you.* This may sound like "turning the other cheek," and that may be the case. We do not do any good for ourselves or our organizations by echoing negativity and bad manners. I like to end calls with difficult people with the phrase "Thank you for your courtesy." Now, I know this probably sounds sarcastic to you. It is imperative that you do not say it sarcastically. Say it as if you mean it. When you do, several things might happen. First, you will feel better about yourself and what you do because the last word in the conversation was positive, and you said it. You will probably be much more inclined to greet the next caller with enthusiasm, as a result. Chances are the other party will think you are being sincere, will take what you said as a compliment, and will admire your good taste in being complimentary toward such a person as him or her. Everybody wins!

17. *Discontinue noisy activities when answering the phone.* I was on a call not too long ago, and the person on the other end was undeniably munching a lunch between sentences with me. I knew this was the case because the person would seem to encourage me to talk between bites, so more time could be spent in this activity. Obviously, this was inappropriate behavior.

Sometimes we think we can successfully perform two tasks at one time without losing efficiency. Some folks make it a practice to use the typewriter while having a phone conversation on an unrelated subject. The noise that the typewriter can introduce into the communication channel should be a sufficient deterrent to this activity.

18. *Avoid leaving a phone off the hook and unattended for any lengthy period of time.* The "open line" is a very dangerous pipeline from your company to the world. There is a great chance that your officemates may decide to have a critical chat

about the company's best account. Their language might be extremely negative, and there could be profanity used. Imagine that all this could occur while your best client was on the open line! It could be more than embarrassing. It could be fatal to one's career!

If you are leaving the line, either place the party on hold or promise to call back. This will diminish the possibility of costly gaffes.

19. *If the boss or an associate gets a call when you are in his/her office, sense if the call is personal or professional. If it is personal, the best idea is to leave. If professional, stay.* You do not have to be a mind reader, in most cases, to determine whether a call is personal. If, all of a sudden, the tones get breathy, and your associate begins to turn red, you have a clue that the call is one you should not be privy to, and you should leave. It is a good idea, if you leave, to stay nearby to resume the conversation.

20. *Discontinue conversations with officemates and other people in your office when you answer the phone.* I am constantly impressed with the number of folks who believe they can successfully carry on two conversations at the same time! When I call them, they answer the phone while speaking to someone in their physical presence. This gets our conversation off to a shaky start because I am waiting in the wings for my turn to speak and be addressed. I sense that some folks actually do this "simulcast" on purpose, in order to appear busy to the person on the phone. To me, they sound like poor time managers and inconsiderate communicators.

21. *Avoid giving the impression to others that you are rushing them off the line.* There is an old expression: "I felt like I was being given the bum's rush!" Most of us have very negative associations with being rushed. We usually feel we are being treated as inferiors and that our concerns are unimportant. When we bruise people's egos in this fashion, they often go out of their way to show us how important they really are! This involves demanding we pay more attention to them, which can be costly for our companies and ourselves.

To Screen or Not to Screen Calls

One of the most controversial, yet commonplace telephone communication practices is the screening of calls by secretaries and others. From the point of view of the executive who chooses to have his/her calls filtered in this way, it is a matter of time and resource management. He or she only has a limited amount of time and an unlimited number of folks who want segments of it. Without posting a "lion at the gate," the executive might be spending so much time with time-wasters as to never get down to the work he or she is paid to do.

The secretary may be instructed to send all calls through except those from "Frank Smith, and all salespeople!" When the phone rings, and the executive is requested, the secretary will use one of a limited number of stock phrases to determine whether the caller is on the "good" or "bad" list. Then the call is routed to the executive, or a message is taken after the caller has been politely discouraged. In principle, screening is a straightforward office function. Why does it cause so much hassle, then?

Callers often complain that they are made to feel "worthless" by the screening process. They have this image that their name and company affiliation are being evaluated superficially and that they are being prevented from conducting legitimate business with the desired party. It is a fact of life that they are often "being kept out" by the secretary, the executive, or both. How can both sides win this game?

Diplomatic Screening Techniques

I believe most callers understand that screening serves a necessary function. Their complaint is that the screening they are put through is an indelicate process. How may we spare the caller a little embarrassment while still getting information from him or her? Commonly, screening proceeds as follows:

Caller: *May I speak with Tracy Jones, please?*

Office: *Who is calling?*

Caller: *This is Frances Smith.*

Office: *And what is this in regard to?*

Caller: *A business matter.*

Office: *Have you spoken with Tracy Jones before?*

Caller: *No, but we've had correspondence.*

Office: [*coolly*] *One moment. I'll see if she's in.* [*after a pause of ten seconds or so*] *I'm sorry, Ms. Jones is away from her desk at this point.* [*no offer of taking a message*]

Caller: *I'll call back. Can you recommend a time at which I can reach her?*

Office: *It's hard to say.*

Caller: [*growing perturbed*] *Would you say she is likely to return to the office today or tomorrow?*

Office: [*echoing the caller's negativity*] *Certainly. I simply cannot predict a specific time. You might try the morning.*

Caller: [*frustrated, disgruntled, defensive*] *Sure.*

Office: *Thanks for calling Acme!*

At this point some readers must be asking, "What's wrong with that call? The office has a right to screen calls, doesn't it?" My answer is yes. The problem with the handling of the caller is that she was made to feel belittled by the "war of attrition" waged by the office. The office asked if she had "spoken with Tracy Jones before." This question might be of minor relevance, but it is largely unnecessary and none of the business of the person requesting the information. Moreover, through this lengthy qualifying procedure, the caller is made to feel that Tracy Jones is definitely in the office, but may elect to "step out" for the purpose of this call. Such evasive tactics tend to make callers defensive. This response can also make the office seem cold and overly forbidding to outsiders.

One technique that is used to soften the harshness of screening is to introduce a little polite language into the process. Instead of saying, for example, "Who is calling?" the office may ask, "And may I tell him/her who is calling, please?" This "telling him/her" phrase indicates that the purpose of the question is to facilitate and not block the routing of the call. The "may I" and "please" phrases are well received also.

I prefer screening by way of changing the script a little. Instead of asking for the person's name, business affiliation, and calling history with a given person, I like to condense these questions into one request: "May I reference this call for you?" This phrase is used by some secretaries at a major corporation, and they have reported that it works very effectively. Here is an example of the phrase in action:

Caller: *May I speak with Tracy Jones, please?*

Office: *May I reference this call for you?*

Caller: *What?*

Office: [*politely and helpfully*] *And may I reference this call for you?*

Caller: *Oh, sure. This is Frances Smith, and I am following up on some correspondence with Tracy.*

Office: *I'll check to see if Ms. Jones is available. Will you hold, please?*

Caller: *Sure.*

Office: *Thank you.* [*returning after a few seconds*] *I'm sorry, Ms. Smith, she is apparently away from her desk right now. May I ask her to return your call, or would you prefer to call back?*

Caller: *I will call back. Thank you.*

Office: *You're welcome. Bye.*

Instead of creating an adversary relationship, which most screening accomplishes, this approach tells the caller that the office is *trying to put the two parties together, if possible, and not keep them apart.* The phrase "May I reference this call for you?" will probably catch the caller by surprise at first, as the example shows. After he or she hears it again, the caller will appreciate that the question is requesting information in a supportive, rather than defensive, manner. The words "for you" indicate that the question is designed to assist the caller by conveying relevant information. It is a whole different feeling from, "May I extract information from you, which I will use against you?" which many screeners imply by their words and tones of voice.

Note the phrase "I'll check to see if Ms. Jones is available." I like to use the word "available" because it more clearly describes the status of the pursued person. He or she may be physically present, but unavailable. The phrase is also appropriate if he or she is not at that physical location. It enables the screener to avoid telling "one more little lie," which he or she should find relieving. It also does not disclose the location of the principal, which can be desirable from a competitive or security perspective. Why tell your competition that the business is expanding to a new region by mentioning unnecessarily that an executive is spending a good deal of time there?

There is another helpful phrase introduced into this example: "May I ask her to return your call, or would you prefer to call back?" This not only might save the time of the principal but also offers a choice to the caller, which is a helpful touch. Further, the taker of the call promises to *ask* the associate to call back rather than *telling* him/her to return the call. Most of us cannot force another person to make calls at a given time. We also execute our responsibility to the caller when we *ask* the person to return the call, irrespective of whether he or she elects to do so.

Transferring Calls Effectively

As mentioned elsewhere, transferring calls can create or add to ill will between ourselves and our clients. If we transfer a person to another extension, and we are not convinced he or she will find help at that station, we are contributing to inefficiency. We are also reducing the productivity of our associates, who may very well know less about the matter of the call then we do.

I propose a rule: *Never transfer a call to another extension simply to get rid of the caller. This form of "hot potato" from one station to another may be eliminated if we take the responsibility to investigate which party might be most likely to be able to assist the caller before we make the transfer.* This may require that we temporarily place the caller on hold or call the person back. In either case the caller will appreciate the effort and efficiency, and we will learn more about the organization for future occasions.

When transferring a call, exercise great care not to disconnect the party; ask permission of the party to make the transfer; tell the reason for the transfer; and give the caller the number of the new extension in case there is a disconnection.

Setting Professional Office Appointments

Most executives and other professionals work by an appointment system, whereby they elect to see prospective clients and suppliers during clearly delineated times. Broken appointments are costly, and those whose responsibility it is to set appointments for the principals appreciate that there is some persuasion involved in "selling" others on certain appointment times, as well as convincing them to honor the commitment they have made. How may we set better appointments?

I think one of the most valuable attitudes that we can convey to our clients and suppliers is that there is a scarcity of time available to all, because of the "popularity" and success of our principal. In conveying this image, we are giving our office a certain degree of credibility, respect, and power, even if our calendars are relatively empty. A common error made by those who set appointments for others is to open up their appointment books to the whims and free choice of the caller. "When would you like to come in?" is a phrase that suggests, "Pick any old time; we have nothing better to do than wait for you to come by!"

We should offer the caller only *a few choices of appointment times, which are convenient to our office.* By limiting the choices we reduce the risk of confusing the caller with too many options, which can make them waste valuable telephone time in the decision-making process. If we do not limit the available appointment times, we inadvertently convey the impression that it is all right to break appointments because new ones are available and are easily made.

I like to use the following sort of phrase to encourage appointments during certain periods. "Fine, Ms. Jones. Our calendar suggests a good time to get together would be Tuesday morning at three o'clock;

or would Wednesday morning at ten be better for you?" For those of you who are familiar with sales calls, you may have noticed that this method of setting appointments utilizes the "choice close." In other words, we are giving the party a specific choice of alternatives, and in doing this, we are likely to fill the time slots we have available. You may have found the phrase "our calendar suggests" to be a bit new in your experience. I have found this phrase extremely helpful because it makes my calendar appear to "do the suggesting," and not myself. Folks are less inclined to disagree with a calendar than they are with another person.

What happens when the party agrees to come in at a certain time, or to see us in their office at a given hour? Do we simply say good-bye and release the line? No. We need to bolster the commitment to the appointment by confirming the understanding that has been reached. Without a confirmation, we do not have the sort of strong appointment we should have. The phrasing of the confirmation is simple. "Fine, Ms. Jones, just so we are clear, we will look forward to seeing you at two o'clock on Thursday, January 12. Thanks very much. Good-bye." This short epilogue signals the other party that we are taking the appointment seriously and that there is an acknowledged agreement to meet.

Some people ask if it is a good idea to mention that the other party should call us if he or she is going to have to miss the appointment. This would be courteous and helpful. I believe most folks understand that appointments should be rescheduled promptly and that missed appointments are inconvenient and costly. I am reluctant to mention that folks should call us if there is a change in plan because this "escape clause" can create the outcome we wish to avoid. It might *suggest that cancellation is acceptable or stimulate a cancellation.* We may be better off by implying that the meeting is somewhat serious and *inconvenient* to cancel or reschedule.

Some offices make it a point to call parties who are scheduled for the next day in order to remind them of their appointment. Where there is competition for few appointment times, and a substantial waiting list for attention, I think this practice is a good idea. Physicians and dentists find the reminder call a great help.

Collecting Unpaid Accounts

In these times of inflation and high interest rates, all businesses are confronted with the need to increase the speed with which they receive funds due them. Many business failures can be chalked up to insufficient "cash flow" to meet present obligations. To avoid troubles along this line, we should explore briefly a few techniques that can help us to recover receivables.

One of the most common collection efforts is made through the device of the *reminder call*. This is the situation. We have a number of accounts on a thirty-day billing, and we have not seen any funds for a period of forty days. What should we do? We appreciate that these accounts are our "bread and butter," and we are reluctant to discourage future trade with them.

I suggest we give them a brief reminder call to make them aware of the situation. Sometimes the client overlooks the invoice. Other times the client may be playing the money market with our funds, waiting for us to remind them of the invoice. Here is an approach we can take that is mild, yet to the point.

> Caller: *Hello, Mr. Smith? This is John Jones with Acme Refrigeration. How are you today? Good. Mr. Smith, the reason I am on the phone is that I have an unpaid invoice in front of me which we sent to your firm about forty days ago. I wanted to make sure you received that.*
>
> Smith: *Yes, we got that.*
>
> Caller: *Will you folks be remitting that within the next few days, then?*
>
> Smith: *Yes, I suppose so.*
>
> Caller: *Well, we will appreciate it. Given the speed of the mails, I should be getting that no later than the end of the week, am I right?*
>
> Smith: *I guess so.*
>
> Caller: *Good. I'll make a point to get back with you on Friday if there are any delays, okay?*

Smith: *Okay.*

Caller: *Thank you for taking care of that for us, Mr. Smith.*

What we are trying to do in a reminder call is gain some sort of commitment to paying by a certain date, while indicating that we won't forget the matter if we fail to see a check. All of this needs to be done with a mild tone of voice, and without any sense of threat to the other party. We are trying to get a slow payer to pay a little faster, not hunt down someone who is trying to stiff us.

Some accounts do turn delinquent, however. With them, we need to be a little more assertive about collecting the bill. We may suspect there is not much chance of turning them back into good clients, but we wish to have them return certain equipment or unused portions of stock we have tendered to them. Our approach, in this case, is more direct.

Caller: *Hello, Mr. Smith? This is Mr. Jones with Acme Refrigeration calling about your overdue bill in the amount of $5,280. When shall we expect payment on this?*

Smith: *Pretty soon.*

Caller: *That sounds good. We need to work out a definite time in which to see payment on this. What do you propose?*

Smith: *Well, I think I can send you something around the first of the month.*

Caller: *Will that be the amount owed?*

Smith: *No, just a part of it.*

Caller: *How much do you plan to pay?*

Smith: *A thousand dollars.*

Caller: *Can you make that two thousand? Then you can retire almost half of your debt.*

Smith: *I'll try.*

Caller: *Will you be able to pay an additional thousand every two weeks?*

Smith: *I think so.*

Caller: *Fine. What we'll do is put you down for a two-thousand-dollar payment on the first, and one thousand dollars every two weeks, until this is paid off. That will be no later than March 25, am I right?*

Smith: *Yeah, that sounds all right.*

Caller: *Fine, Mr. Smith. We will count on seeing your check on the first. If we don't, we'll be in touch with you again.*

Smith: *Okay.*

Caller: *Thank you, Mr. Smith.*

Some of this dramatized call may violate the "norm" in commercial collection circles, but this approach does make the demand for payment while allowing for the sort of flexibility that will make payment likely. We do not want to turn off the other party to such an extent that he or she says, "Take me to court, then!" If this happens, everyone loses.

You will note that I asked what the other person "proposes" in terms of paying the bill. Often folks will go out of their way to generate an acceptable payment program if they are given the opportunity. If we force upon them an inflexible program, they are likely to reject it, and we don't see our money.

Sometimes our contacts within organizations "cop out" by saying, "Well, you know how slow big companies are in paying their bills!" This kind of evasion must be met with a personal appeal from us to our counterpart. "I recognize that, Tracy. That's why I am going to ask you to look into the matter to see where we are in the process. Who knows, they may have lost the invoice! May I count on you to shepherd this thing through for me?" Invariably, the person will help us out to some extent.

By improving professional office telecommunications we will assure our companies of better profits, improved public relations, and smoother operations. We will also better serve our clients and communities.

6

Fighting Back: The Consumer's Guide to the Telephone

When Lyndon Johnson was President, in the 1960s, football was becoming, if not the national pastime, the nation's passion. Super Bowls created excitement across the land. They were viewed by record-breaking numbers on television, although only a privileged few were lucky or wealthy enough to see the games in person.

A "typical consumer," living in Texas during this time, thought he should be able to go to a game of the magnitude of the Super Bowl. He started telling his friends that he was going to find a way to get tickets to the forthcoming championship game, though the game had been sold out for months. His friends, being of ordinary financial means as well, dismissed his proclaimed intention as fantasy.

As the Super Bowl week approached, our consumer was reading the local newspaper and found an article that said President Johnson was ill and had been taken to the Bethesda Naval Hospital for tests, which would last for several days. All of a sudden, in a flash of insight, the consumer said to himself: "The President of the United States always has a ticket to the big games in baseball and football! I'll bet *he* has a Super Bowl ticket that will just go to waste because he can't go." Figuring there wasn't much time before the day of the game, the consumer picked up the phone and placed a call to the President at the hospital. He didn't get to speak with him personally, of course, but he left a message. He said he deeply regretted the President's condition, but if the President couldn't make the game, perhaps he could do a "loyal constituent a favor" by giving him the ticket. Sure enough, according to legend, the ticket arrived in the consumer's mail within a few days!

What is the moral of this story? Our consumer had the creativity and courage to ask for what he wanted, using the power and directness of the telephone to get it. It is a fact that most savvy consumers and business people appreciate: You may find it impossible to speak with an important man or woman face to face, but you can reach all kinds of significant people by telephone and get action from them quickly.

Speaking With Celebrities and Other "Untouchables"

On a lark, a college buddy and I decided to make the twelve-hour drive from Los Angeles to Lake Tahoe, Nevada, one weekend. Instead of making advance hotel reservations, we just figured we would try our luck and see what was available. We drove to the North Shore, which I understood to be the most recreational and beautiful part of the lake. We became increasingly disconsolate as we saw one "no vacancy" sign after another. Suddenly, I remembered that my dad knew the owner of a large hotel and casino. I thought my friend and I had nothing to lose by using this ace in the hole. Upon arriving at the beautiful spot, we were told that the hotel had no rooms. I asked for the manager of the hotel and told him that the owner would probably wish us to be accommodated. The manager insisted he had no rooms. I said, "I know you have to be holding a suite or two for V.I.P.s, and we will be happy to use one of them, at a reasonable rate, of course." I then asked him to get the owner on the phone and explain the situation. He tried, to no avail. Judging us to be "authentic," the manager conceded that he did have "half of a suite available, which consists of a bedroom, with a large bed, and a living room with a convertible sofa." He said he would give us these rooms at a fraction of their regular cost. We grabbed the offer.

Upon arriving in the room, we found it beautifully appointed, with two large color TVs, a wet bar, and a commanding view of forest and lake. It even had a French phone in the bathroom! I asked my buddy what he wanted to do for entertainment. He mentioned seeing a billboard that advertised the Jonathan Winters show at the Sahara, on the other side of the lake. I placed a call to the hotel and was told that his show was sold out. Feeling a little low, but not defeated, I decided to see if Jonathan Winters himself could do something for us!

At this point, my friend thought I was nuts. I called the Sahara and asked for "Mr. Winters' room, please." A voice that I did not recognize came on the line and said, "Mr. Winters' room." I said, "Gary Goodman for Mr. Winters, please." The voice responded, "One minute, please." The next voice I heard was Jonathan Winters'! I couldn't believe it. He was on the line, for little old me! I said, "Mr. Winters, my friend and I are here from Los Angeles, and we are great fans of yours. We have been told that the show is sold out, and we thought you might be able to do something for us. Perhaps you could set up a few chairs backstage or something." He replied with a very kind tone of voice, "Gary, I'm sorry. In the last half hour about thirty of my friends have called me to see the show, and I simply can't fit anyone else in. It's too bad tonight is my last show here this trip." I thanked him and got off the line.

My friend was totally thrilled by this conversation. He asked, "What did he say?" I told him Jonathan Winters apologized for not being able to accommodate us. That's right: *apologized!* Mr. Winters' gracious manner with me was a surprise to me at that point, but I have found time and again that folks of his stature are *not only accessible to us by telephone but are often pleased to speak to us!*

Do Your Calling the "Beverly Hills Way"

I had the good fortune to have been brought up for a part of my youth in the famous city of Beverly Hills, California. I cannot minimize the impact of this environment upon my view of what can be accomplished by telephone. I think I probably had one of the best "role models" in my father, who was involved in the radio, television, and advertising industries.

His approach to solving a problem or seizing an opportunity was to pick up the phone! Indeed, he had a marvelous way of establishing rapport with others while achieving his objectives through this medium.

He was *fearless.* As a businessman he would use the phone to network with influential counterparts, and as a consumer he would take his troubles to the top through this medium.

To use Rodney Dangerfield's phrase, my father got "respect" when he used the phone. What were some of his secrets as well as those used by Beverly Hills people?

You're Important! Now Sound That Way!

I think the number-one thing that powerful folks cultivate is a *forceful telephone personality.* They make it sound as though they are using the telephone because they simply do not have time to write a letter of complaint or inquiry. They are important enough to require immediate attention, in other words. One of the most effective approaches to solving a problem as a consumer is to make the other party feel that "your voice counts," and behind you stands "an army" of other complainers who will rattle some cages if you do not obtain justice.

How to Complain by Telephone, and Win!

When consumers have a complaint to make with a vendor, whether it is a manufacturer or retailer, they tend to make several mistakes, which should be avoided.

1. *They delay making their feelings known because they don't want to be considered a complainer or be disliked.* Most of us expect trouble of one sort or another when we are about to make a complaint or request for service. Anticipating lengthy delays and surly personalities, we put off until another day or year what is our right to do this minute. *Strike while the iron is hot!* If you just purchased an item in a department store, for instance, and you find it does not function as it should, get on the phone right away. You might be able to speak with the salesperson who helped you. This person can make an exchange or refund easier for you than a person in the accounting department. You may find that returning the item right away can save you from the prospect of added grief in trying to remove the charge from your credit card later.

Do not be discouraged by poor treatment. Expect it and deal

with it effectively. It is an unfortunate fact that most businesses have poorly trained telephone help, and when you need attention, you will invariably get one of these folks to help you. Chances are they will be defensive with you, and will perceive your complaint as a personal attack, or will refuse to give your case any special treatment; which means you will get satisfaction no sooner than the return of Halley's comet.

2. *Consumers believe that "anyone" can and will help them with their problem.* As mentioned above, the "help" at many firms may be less than noteworthy. To avoid poor treatment, *go straight to the top!* Ask for the manager of the offending department or the president or owner of the company. These folks are paid to make sure the organization is spared embarrassment and poor public relations. Too often the lowly clerk is unconcerned and can even obstruct your request for better goods and services. It is true that the president of the firm may refer you to another functionary, but you will be operating from a position of greater strength when you reach him or her. You should start your lament with the words: "Mr./Ms. President suggested I speak with you. He/she said you would be able to help me with this matter." This prelude is a nice way of saying: "Look, Jack. President Blank is going to follow up on this case, so you had better treat me seriously unless you want your head to roll." The person will get the message.

3. *Consumers allow their emotions to make Jell-O of their reasoning powers.* Few things turn off professional complaint recipients more than an overwrought consumer whose emotions are out of control. If you wish to get action from an agency, you need to organize your ideas and demands before you get on the phone. The PEP Format, discussed in detail in Chapter 3, is ideal for framing your request or demand.

> You: *My name is Tracy Smith, and I require a refund for the widget I purchased at your store today. It doesn't work correctly. It wasn't the color I wanted. It is overpriced. I require a refund. How will this be expedited?*
>
> Them: *Can you bring it back in?*
>
> You: *No. I have already made a wasted trip, which is very costly to me. Your delivery truck can pick up the item between noon*

and five this afternoon and give me a receipt. I will expect a refund check by mail. You will need my address, right?

Them: *Well, hold on for a minute. I'll have to find out if we can do that, okay?*

You: *I'll wait for one minute, thank you.*

Them: [*getting back on the line*] *What did you say your address was?*

Note how "You" handled this call. Was there any question who was in control of the conversation from beginning to end? Each phrase was simple and to the point. There was a specific demand for action made by the consumer, and certain conditions placed on how the complaint was going to be handled. You probably found the demand for a pickup rather gutsy. It is. But when you really think about the waste involved in having to go to a store twice, simply to be restored to the condition you were in before you went, you will conclude that you have a right to a little service at this point.

There is a cold, logical tone to the demand that the consumer made in this example. This is effective because it suggests power. The consumer obviously knows what his or her "rights" are, and the serious tone signals the offenders that they should not try any evasive or inconvenient tactics.

4. *Consumers are victimized by their own civility.* If a firm can make us feel "guilty" about complaining, then they can get us to accept a remedy that is more in their interest than ours. Many firms try to "shame" us into being more generous with their errors than we should be. Growing up, as we do, in a "civil" society, which values forgiveness, we are likely to take the bait and get hung up by our own manners. Showing anger is considered undignified, and so we tend to avoid this at all costs. Are we causing ourselves more problems by being so civil? I think so, in some cases.

I was using a supplier for a period of time, and he seemed incapable of getting the simplest orders right. When I would complain, I would go out of my way not to hurt his feelings, as I recognize my proclivity for sounding powerful on the phone. Repeatedly, he'd blow my orders, though. One day I determined he wasn't taking me seriously because I was so "nice and understanding." I decided, as the old expression says, "No more Mr. Nice Guy!" I got him on the phone and said, "Look. I've had enough of this incompetence. Either you get these orders straight, or I am going to sue you for all the money and misery our association has cost me!" My voice was much more threatening than it had ever been with him. I was allowing myself to show a little rage. I was still under control emotionally, but I let it be known that my anger would be diminished only through quick action of the remedial or legal variety. He got the point. I never had another problem with him.

If I had continued being civil with him, I would have been giving tacit approval to dismal treatment. We should show our "righteous indignation" toward an organization when more polite channels are unsuccessful. This does not suggest we should be overly emotional. We should add a certain degree of force and conviction to our "logic."

5. *Consumers are unaware of "courts of higher authority" to which they can bring a complaint and gain a better chance of succeeding.* Most modern businesses, including the largest in given industries, belong to professional and trade associations. These organizations have as one of their missions the safeguarding of the "public image" of member firms. Consequently, committees and bureaus are set up by the national, state, or regional group to "police" its members in respect to trade practices. If a complaint is made by telephone to one of these organizations, pressure can be swiftly brought to bear upon an offending member. If the firm with which you have trouble is a local concern, perhaps the best place to start is to lodge a complaint with the local Better Business Bureau, to be found in your telephone directory. It is probable that your claim will have to be recorded in writing, but you can determine your rights and chances for success by consulting the bureau by telephone. Your public library is a tremendous resource for consulting directories of associations and trade groups where complaints can be lodged. Remember, if it seems that an organization is uncooperative with you, there are other avenues of redress available to you.

6. *Consumers are reluctant to "go public" with the problem, or threaten to do the same.* Sometimes we need to "shock" an agency into doing what it should have done all along. One of the best gambits is to promise the offending firm that you are going to make a complaint to one of the media "action lines" in your town. The prospect of news

crews invading their corporate turf will make even the most recalcitrant people cooperate in getting us off their backs.

If the offender does not respond, be prepared to follow through on your promise. Call the producer of the show, be it radio or television, and tell your story in a dispassionate way. Try to assert that your complaint is probably one of many that others would make if they could be heard. By showing yourself to be a victim of a larger class of persons, you will be taken more seriously, and your complaint will have a greater likelihood of being handled.

7. *Consumers believe that by asking for less, they are more likely to be treated reasonably.* This is a false proposition for a few reasons. First, folks are much more likely to pay attention to a matter when it seems that there is something of magnitude at stake. If we make our complaint seem inconsequential, we are likely to persuade others to ignore the matter. Second, behavioral research tells us that the greater the attitude change asked for, the greater the likelihood that we will get *some* of what we are asking for. Ask for a pittance, and you will be lucky to get it. Ask for the moon, and you will stand a better chance of getting more than you thought you would get.

A fellow I used to teach with ordered a table and chairs from a nationally known retail chain store. Upon inspection after delivery, my friend found a number of small nicks in the finish of the table. The chairs arrived unscathed. He called the customer service department of the store and asked for the manager. Explaining the situation, my friend indicated his dissatisfaction with the condition of the furniture. The manager asked, "What would you like us to do?" Sensing an opportunity, my friend reasoned: "Well, if you have to deliver another set and retrieve this one, it will cost you guys about a hundred bucks, I would think. That's close to the cost of the entire set! If you will take off twenty percent from the price of the goods, I will accept them, as is, and consider the matter over." The manager considered the proposition and agreed to rebate 20 percent of the purchase price and record the amount on my friend's charge account.

Many consumers would have looked at this situation and concluded that both the retailer and consumer were bound to lose. My friend confided to me that he would have been pleased with a 10 percent rebate and was thrilled to get 20. He asked for more, and he got it!

8. *Consumers hear "no" for an answer and believe it.* Persistence and assertiveness are behaviors that the savvy consumer cultivates. Winning by telephone requires we "toughen" ourselves so we will not be easy to pass off or rebuff.

I was doing some business in the Toledo area, and my schedule called for me to stay in town until a Saturday evening. Suddenly, my plans changed during the tour, and I had to alter my airline reservation. I phoned the airline and was told that there wouldn't be any problem in getting on the Friday evening flight, although there was only one flight available. Sensing that something might go wrong, I asked for reassurance from the reservations person that I had a confirmed change of reservation. I even made a point of asking the name and employee number of the person with whom I was speaking, and I asked whether I could refer to the employee if anything went wrong with my reservation. Yes, yes, yes. I hung up the phone and took myself to dinner in my hotel. Afterward, I had a strong urge to call the airline and reconfirm my passage. I called, and they *had no record of my change in reservations! The flight I needed was also booked at that point!*

I used practically every tip I have mentioned in these pages to deal with the situation. I insisted upon speaking with the highest-ranking official in the airline "immediately." This turned out to be a supervisor in Cincinnati. The person assured me that she understood how I felt, but could not get me on the flight. I referred to my initial conversation that evening with the reservations agent and indicated that I had been promised space on the plane. She again "understood how I felt." I insisted that it wasn't fair that I could be so terribly misled. She "understood how I felt," but . . . Finally, I decided I had been mollified enough. I retorted:

"You do not *understand how I feel* because if you did, you wouldn't use the same old transition phrase on me. Can't your people teach you folks a few different ways to say no besides 'I understand how you feel, but . . .'? What about, 'I know what you mean, but,' or 'I understand that, but'; anything but 'I understand how you feel"!

She actually responded with this phrase again, as if I had been speaking to a brick wall. I decided to "go for the gusto" at that point. I said something to the effect: "Look, I know you can get me on that plane if you have to. I am telling you that you *have to*. Either I get on that plane, or the C.A.B. [Civil Aeronautics Board] will hear about this and you will have to answer for it! I will not get off this line until you assure me that when I present myself for boarding Friday evening, I will be ushered directly to the plane. Now, if you do not have the authority to make this determination, I will wait on this line to speak to someone who can."

It worked. I was exhausted, but I did get on the plane. The moral of the story is to refuse to take no for an answer if you strongly believe you can be accommodated. Remember one thing: Behavioral research suggests that we have the ability to come across the phone stronger than we do in person. Consequently, using the telephone to lodge a complaint or get satisfaction can be a wiser thing to do than taking up our cause in person. A person may discount our looks, but find it hard to belittle us when we are coming through the earpiece loud and clear.

There is another important lesson in that episode. Someone, somewhere, has the authority to modify a rule or pave your way to satisfaction. This principle applies to public agencies, which promote an image of inflexibility and invincibility, as well as to private firms. Somebody can bend the rules for you, if you find that person. Do not let the lions and bozos at the gate discourage your quest for that person. I like to pose the following "qualifying question" to an underling: "Who has the authority to say yes to me?" The person may not tell you right away. Never fear. Simply repeat your question. You will get the name, and then ask to be connected with that party. When that person comes on the line, say: "I understand you have the authority to override the XYZ procedure, am I right?" After hearing a positive response, tell the person your wish. If the person says no, he or she does not have authority, find out who does. Then proceed with your complaint.

9. *Consumers believe they must wage their battles alone, without help.* There are few things as powerful and effective as accessing professional help to assist in winning battles. Many professions use the telephone as a pugilistic device, including lawyers, negotiators, and talent agents. If you have a friend who is strong on the phone, you might

ask him or her to make a few calls on your behalf, and you can reciprocate when that person has a few battles to fight. When a proxy calls for us, we seem to be more powerful to the offending agency because we are not alone. This teamwork can do wonders. You can, of course, resort to an attorney, who can make a call on your behalf. While this service may cost you a small sum, it can shake up the opposition enough to motivate the kind of action you want. (We will also discuss some free services that consumers can access, including legal services, in a later section.)

10. *Consumers fail to document their transactions, including telephone conversations.* "Did you keep your receipt?" is a question we hear whenever we try to make an exchange or return of an item. Surprisingly few folks take this simple precaution when making a purchase. It is, of course, invaluable to have proof-of-purchase documentation available for reference throughout the complaint process.

It is also important to make notes of all of the names of people with whom you speak in reference to a matter, as well as to the representations made and the subjects discussed. Should any legal action take place, you will be well served by your records of calls.

It is also good practice to make a telephone complaint *and follow it up the same day with a brief letter referring to your conversation.* This lends further authenticity to your claim because you are obviously taking the time to communicate through different avenues. By using the media of letters and telephone you will lend momentum to your cause. There is an assumption made by agencies that it takes more time and commitment to a cause to put it into writing, so the combination of phone call and letter will have the effect of "blasting 'em with both barrels."

Free Services Available by Telephone

With the increasing costs of fuel and inflation, more and more agencies are appearing that offer free or low-cost services to consumers who are aware of them. Additionally, conventional firms can be called upon to give a certain amount of professional advice and counseling by telephone, at no cost to the caller. Here are some of the services available.

Legal Advice

Lawyers and other professionals are careful not to "give away" their ideas to callers for free, yet they obtain much of their business by convincing the caller that they have answers to their problems. What this means is most attorneys are going to hear your problem before determining whether they can be of assistance. Thus, you have an opportunity to find out: (1) whether a matter is worth pursuing, from a legal point of view; (2) how it might be pursued, through formal or less formal legal channels; and (3) how much the matter will cost. Armed with this information, as well as a certain amount of legal analysis, you can decide to pursue the matter independently or with an attorney. As will be mentioned in a later section, the telephone is a marvelous means of *comparison shopping. We should comparison shop nearly everything by telephone, including professional services.* When it comes to spending your dollars, little should be sacred and excluded from comparison shopping.

Many credit unions and other associations offer free telephone advice from attorneys associated with a given firm. Some relationships are with a number of firms across the country, which enables members to find legal help no matter where they are. I was doing some shopping in another state during the summer when a legal question arose between a local merchant and myself. He asserted that there was a charge for state tax on all items sold within the state, including those items that were going to be shipped out of state. I disagreed with this view. In order to test our theories, I asked to use his telephone to call my attorneys. He couldn't believe the length to which this "crazy Californian" was going to prove a point. I took my legal services card from my wallet, which had been supplied by my credit union, and I dialed an 800 number appropriate for that state. Within minutes I was speaking with an attorney. She gave me her opinion on the matter, and the issue was swiftly settled.

I have found that legal advice and information from other professionals may most easily be obtained if the consumer has narrowed the issue about which he or she is concerned to one or a few "yes and no" questions. "Would it be worth it to pursue a matter whereby someone did XYZ to me?" By asking a question in this manner we can certainly get the answer we are looking for, and also obtain the ordinarily costly "professional reasoning" that might be withheld from a less savvy questioner. The party will also respect our economy in asking for specific information.

Psychological Advice

Psychological "hot lines" have been available in most major cities for several years. Often operated by local "free clinics" or area hospitals, these agencies are staffed by people who are trained to handle "crisis" calls, as well as less urgent communications. These units make available counseling to folks who may not have the financial means or motivation to seek private or extended attention.

Medical Hot Lines

Numbers of medical hot lines exist to help callers. In Los Angeles, for instance, the local American Medical Association chapter offers a medical referral service to callers, as well as the resources of a medical librarian who can explore certain subjects for doctors. The University of Southern California Student Health Center provides a telephone service in which people can inquire about various medical and dental conditions and hear taped messages about particular subjects of interest. This is a particularly valuable free service because folks can ask to hear a recording without undergoing the embarrassment associated with speaking to a "live" person about the condition. "V.D." hot lines have become popular sources of free information as well.

Telephone directories and local community agencies are some of the best places to start building a list of hot-line phone numbers. They are extremely valuable sources of information in both critical and everyday situations.

Talk-Radio Can Save You Money!

One of the most interesting uses of the telephone is made by radio stations that offer phone-in programs, where we can speak with experts on various subjects. Except for the cost of the call, in most cases we can address people whom we could never afford otherwise. I have spoken with several people who have been helped with everything from family advice to car repair by radio.

There is one person who makes a point of calling radio stations to determine if they have any free tickets that week. Because media sources sponsor or are associated with concerts, plays, and sporting events, they often have free or complimentary tickets, which they give away over the air, or fail to give away. This woman goes to a major event every other week, it seems, by simply calling the station during and between contests.

The 800 Bonanza: Discovering Hidden Toll-Free Numbers

There has been an explosion in the use of toll-free 800 numbers within the last few years. Most of the largest corporations have at least one such incoming telephone line for the purpose of accepting orders or fielding customer service problems. Sometimes these helpful phone numbers are not publicized, so the smart consumer explores other avenues to determine whether a particular company has one. First, we can all dial 1-800 555-1212 from any telephone and ask whether a company has such a line. In some cases the company will have a line, but it will be advertised as being connected with some obscure department or corporate function. *Call the number anyway!* The firm may give you another 800 line that is not publicized. You might get lucky in another way. The shipping department may not be the only office connected to the 800 number. There may be extensions throughout the organization, so your call can be easily transferred.

Although it is a little known fact, *there is an 800 number telephone directory, which may be purchased from a private firm.* As of the date of this writing, the directory lists over 800 categories of organizations, including 9,000 hotels and motels and 160 airlines, and claims to offer the "50 most useful toll-free 800 numbers in existence today." For information, write: Landmark Publishing, Box 3287, Burlington, VT 05402.

The advantage to using a directory is that we can contact many companies within a given category and discover firms and organizations of service we would not have known about otherwise. The 800 Information telephone operator will not search a category for us. He or she will only investigate a particular listing if we first provide the name.

Become a Purchasing Pro

Armed with 800 numbers, the consumer can use the entire country as his or her marketplace. This elevates the "civilian" into the lofty and powerful ranks of professional "buyers" of corporations, who commonly use the telephone to access a wide network of potential suppliers to find the best buys. Let's take a quick look at what a consumer can do to increase his/her purchasing power. Most consumers purchase their disposable cleaning and stationery items at retail by going to several neighborhood stores for the respective items. This can be a great waste of time and money. Numbers of businesses will sell to individual consumers on a cash-and-carry basis, as long as the buyer is going to pick up various sizes of "boxes" of goods at one time. Let's say that you purchase a couple of ball-point pens and pads of writing paper every third time you go the market. You also pick up four or eight rolls of bathroom tissue, a few boxes of trash-can liners, and hand soap, among other "small" items. If you went to a paper and industrial supply company once every eight weeks or so, and placed a bulk order, you might save up to 50 percent on these necessities! That adds up over the years.

I suggest you look in your local Yellow Pages for industrial suppliers, janitorial suppliers, and others. If you cannot make a large enough purchase by yourself, form a co-op with neighbors to go in with you on an initial purchase. You will be impressed with your savings.

If you live in a small town, or find it inconvenient to personally pick up your purchases, you will find that most suppliers are prepared to ship items to you if the proper arrangements are made. Consequently, the entire transaction can take place by telephone! It is also wise to remember one fact: Your local supplier or retailer is not necessarily cheaper in prices than a firm that proposes to do business with you across country. Therefore, consider developing relationships with reputable companies *everywhere.* It can save you a bundle.

Price Shopping for the Best Deals

The telephone can also be used to investigate certain products and "price-shop" various sources of supply. Once you have determined what kind of product you are interested in buying, call a number of potential sellers. Mention right away that you are interested in a given model-number device or item, and you are comparing prices. Then ask them directly what they are charging for the item. If they ask you, "What other prices have you heard?" indicate you will tell them "in a minute." If their price sounds high, or you have received a lower quotation, tell them. This is helpful in a few ways. First, suppliers should know when consumers think their prices are high. Pressure creates motivation to revise prices downward. You may then ask them if that's "the best you can do on the item." If you are speaking with a manager or business owner who is hungry for a quick, firm sale, he or she may come down in price *while you are on the phone!* This can only add dollars to your pocketbook.

I know this technique is successful because I have purchased everything from clothes dryers to luxury automobiles by this tele-method. It can actually be fun to pit one supplier against another on a given call. Remember, competition serves the consumer's interest. It is up to us, as sharp telephone communicators, to create competition where none exists and take advantage of what we have created.

Keeping Retailers Honest

Retailers live and die by the response they get from newspaper advertisements. Often they use what are called "loss leaders," or low-priced sale items, to encourage consumers to come into stores. This technique works. We come in to purchase one item on sale, and while we're at it, we pick up a few more that are not specially priced.

Often retailers run out of a limited supply of advertised items. Many offer "rain checks" that allow us to purchase at the reduced price when the item is replenished. This can be a waste of time, gasoline, and money. To save headaches, we should always *call ahead to make sure the store has a sufficient amount of stock of the sale item to warrant a personal trip.* One of the most frequently heard consumer complaints is that sellers run out of advertised items. Don't let this happen to you.

"Reaching Out" . . . for Less Money: Using Ma Bell's Competitors

Because of recent Federal Communication Commission rulings, the Bell Telephone companies have started to face formidable competition from other long-distance companies. Leading the way are such adversaries as MCI Telecommunications and SP Communications, which is one of the Southern Pacific companies. The attraction of these firms is the fact that they offer businesses and consumers rather dramatic savings on long-distance calls, as long as users spend over twenty-five dollars or so per month on long-distance service.

This is how an alternative phone service works. If you live in a major metropolitan area, you dial a toll-free telephone number that connects you with a computer. Upon hearing a tone, you punch in your "access code," which identifies the account to which your call should be billed. You continue to punch in the desired phone number and wait to be connected. The calls you make on an alternative system will be billed to you by that company, and do not appear on your regular phone bill.

There are a few drawbacks to using an alternative phone service. You need to use a touch-tone phone in order to make your calls. If you are like the majority of Americans who do not have touch-tone service right now, you will have to purchase an adaptor unit which will give your rotary phone the capability of generating tones. Computers need to "hear" tones to make sense of your access code and allow you into the network. This purchase will set you back approximately forty dollars (at this time). You do have the privilege of renting a touch-tone phone from the "regular" phone company, at extra charge. Both ways, you incur an added expense.

Another drawback to using these services is that the quality of the telephone connection may be very poor. It has been my personal experience that about 50 percent of the connections are problematic. The main culprit is low volume, whereby others cannot hear me clearly. This could result from the fact that alternative phone services employ a patchwork of facilities in order to route long-distance calls. Calls are sent through satellite or microwave facilities owned by competing phone companies, and are then routed through local phone systems in the area you are calling. The resulting telephonic quality may not be as clear as "Bell."

Nonetheless, if your intention is to call Aunt Minnie every weekend to catch up on recent events, and you intend to visit for an extended period of time, the low-cost alternatives may be for you. *Consumer Reports* compared the costs for different calling periods during weekdays, evenings, and weekends, and found in every case the alternatives were cheaper to use than direct dialing through AT&T.[1] Again, the overall savings will vary depending upon your personal frequency of using long-distance telephone services.

To reach some of the alternative phone services, you may use this list, which contains the name of the company and the telephone number. Some firms, such as MCI, SP Communications, and ITT, have different rates and programs for businesses and consumers. Make sure to tell them the service is for home use because rates are usually lower.

Company	*Phone*
MCI Telecommunications	*Consult Local Directory or: (212) 797-2511*
SP Communications	*Consult Local Directory or: (415) 692-5600*
ITT (not AT&T)	*1-800-221-7267*
Western Union	*1-800-325-1403 (1-800-392-1561 in Missouri)*

The number of vendors is not limited to this list. According to one account, as many as thirty competing companies may be in the field as of this writing. People tell me that some of the "package deals" offered by less well known firms than those mentioned above may be suspect. I advise you ask for a list of satisfied customers if you run across one of the newer firms.

Gather Information Quickly and Resourcefully

There is probably no better instrument though which the average person may obtain information than the telephone. By picking up the phone we can be in almost instant contact with any expert the world over. Few of us use the instrument to its fullest, however.

Networking with Others

The "w hen's movement" has popularized the phrase "networking." This is a concept through which folks may contact others who are "experts" or experienced in given areas. By doing so, they can obtain everything from advice to jobs. This activity is facilitated by phone because the "network" does not have to have physical or geographical boundaries. Jane Heim, of Naperville, Illinois, has published a *Directory of Working Women,* which is designed to list the names of working women whom others may contact to obtain advice on professional and career matters. The idea is that those who are listed benefit from exposure, and the callers obviously benefit from speaking with those who know the ropes in various fields.[2]

One doesn't have to be female to enjoy the benefits of networking. I have effectively used the telephone to perform "personal surveys" to test ideas before chairpersons of corporate boards, business consultants, and college professors. The results are dazzling. As mentioned earlier in the chapter, we can gain access to almost anybody by phone.

Using Library Services

With growing concerns over inflation and the costs of government, all kinds of social services have been curtailed in recent years. Perhaps the most near and dear to me has been the public library system. I have used, and continue to use, library services as a "full partner" in my business. To the extent still possible, may I suggest you take advantage of your local library to do likewise for your consumer interests.

Did you know, for example, you can call many local libraries and ask reference librarians to investigate facts and consumer publications for you? If they cannot give you instant answers, they will often call you back with their findings. This can be an immense help, for instance, if you are battling a large company with a complaint, and you need the name of the president of the firm right away. Librarians are pleased to "troubleshoot" areas of investigation for us, and try to discover where we should start in learning about a given area. All this may be just a local call away!

Using the Telephone with Computer Power

Some consumers are becoming so sophisticated that they are hooking up to data bases through a telephone link with a computer. Several sources of data are available. For instance, *The New York Times Index,* which covers numbers of publications over the last several years, may be accessed by telephone and computer, as can data bases in other fields of knowledge. *NASA* data bases contribute scientific know-how for computer retrieval, as do scholarly publications in the social sciences, education, and humanities. Ph.D. dissertations are recorded in a data base known as "Datrix," and one may search this list of titles and key words to determine if any recent investigations would be of value.

While computer information searches may seem a little exotic to you right now, they will probably become much more commonplace in a few years. You may not have to leave your home to obtain the latest information on nearly any subject.

Want to Go into Business for Yourself?

One of the best ways to test an idea is to get a number of opinions other than your own. The phone is a tremendous "polling" mechanism, and we do not have to be Gallups and Harrises to exploit it.

If you have ever thought of going into business for yourself, you probably stumbled over one very real obstacle: Where do you get your sales? Whom do you contact? Through what means? Tele-marketing may be your answer.

Most new businesses invest small fortunes in mailing pieces, expensive stationery, and large offices, before they ever get off the ground. If you wish to start a second-income business or a full-time venture, I suggest you begin by "dialing your way" to profitability.

Contact a number of potential buyers by phone. Ask them if they would be likely to use a product or service such as yours. Keep track of the responses. The tally will give you an approximation of the odds of succeeding. If you get enough encouragement, the next step is to ask for specific orders. You may be surprised to see how many you will get!

The telephone marketing industry is presently a $9-billion enterprise and is growing rapidly. Perhaps the most inviting aspect of marketing through this means is its low capitalization cost and flexibility. If you find you are "riding a winner," it is a rather easy proposition to expand your efforts without sustaining some of the other headaches of growth.

One of the best ways to get started in using the phone for personal development is to become associated with a political or charitable group that engages in fund raising or special events. By asking to start a phone contact campaign, or by joining an existing effort, you can gain valuable experience and determine your aptitude for using the phone in different contexts.

Special Benefits for the Aged and Infirm

As a guest on a recent radio call-in program, I was amazed at the number of elderly and handicapped folks who rely on the telephone as their lifeline to the outside world. According to Professor Deanne Honeyman-Goodman, of California State University, Los Angeles, who is an expert in the communication patterns of the aged, the telephone provides everything from "peace of mind to vital human contact" for the nation's older citizens. She points out that services such as "Dial a Prayer" and "Dial a Ride" are used most frequently by the elderly. Another popular hot-line service is "Call a Friend," through which those confined to their homes may be looked in on by volunteers, in order to safeguard their condition. Those who suffer from visual impairments or limited physical mobility find the telephone an indispensable means of "reaching out," according to the professor.[3]

Overcoming Phone Fear

Many consumers need to confront the challenge of handling their own "call-reluctance" before they can fully utilize the tips offered in this book. A number of you may find you "freeze up" when you think about calling a strange party, or someone calls you whom you have not met before. Don't worry. I have spoken with a number of folks around the country who feel the same way.

One of the main concerns of those who are "phono-phobics" is that they will be negatively judged by the other party based upon voice alone. They think they make a much better impression in person. Second, they are concerned about the way in which another person is responding to their messages because they don't have visual feedback to tell them how their words are doing. Additionally, a number of folks are simply shy and are afraid of new contacts, whether they come over the phone or in person.

There are two basic ways to overcome phone fear: systematic

desensitization and success-imaging. If a person is afraid of water, he or she is instructed to put a toe in the water first, observe that nothing negative transpires, build self-confidence, and venture forth in bolder increments until fully immersed. This sort of gradual or systematic desensitization may be accomplished over the phone as well. Give yourself small telephonic challenges to begin with, pat yourself on the back with minor "victories," and move on to greater challenges. Success-imaging is a process through which we enlist the help of our imagination to overcome our fears. What we do is imagine that we are going to be extremely successful on a given call. We visualize, step by step, the positive feedback we will produce from the other party as the call progresses. We cause ourselves to feel a warm glow of satisfaction that our goal will be accomplished. When we have that "winning expectation," we place our call. The expectation of success will be communicated through our voices, and we will become much more effective as a result.

It does take time to manage phone fear. Like stage fright, which afflicts actors and other performers, we may never completely vanquish our phone fear. This may not be such a bad thing, really. Actors and others report that they "channel" their fear into energy to create inspired performances. Some claim that they are concerned *when they feel no fear because they may give a "flat" performance.* Try to remember to avoid telling yourself you have to be "perfect" on every call in order to be an effective telephone communicator. This kind of self-demand is unrealistic and can lead to procrastination and ineffectiveness. With practice, though, your fears should become much more manageable.

The Great Equalizer

People often ask me in seminars: "Are certain types of people better on the telephone than others?" Having been in telephone communication management for a number of years, I must conclude, "No." The answer to this question is not simply arrived at, however.

All different kinds of folks succeed on the telephone, with the proper attitude and training. This is what is so marvelous about the tool that is currently in nearly every household in the country. We can all become more effective and realize our goals as consumers and businesspeople if we set specific goals for improvement. We don't have to "look the part," or be limited by the countless constraints that inform face-to-face communication. In these respects the telephone can be called "the great equalizer." It is an instrument that holds forth tremendous promise to those who realize its potential.

Notes

1. "Bypassing Ma Bell," *Consumer Reports,* March 1981, p. 167.
2. "Job Network—A Phone Call Away: Book Helps Women Entering the Business World," Los Angeles *Times,* August 27, 1981, Part V, p. 30.
3. Personal interview with Deanne Honeyman-Goodman, California State University, Los Angeles, Speech Communication Department, August 23, 1981.

Index